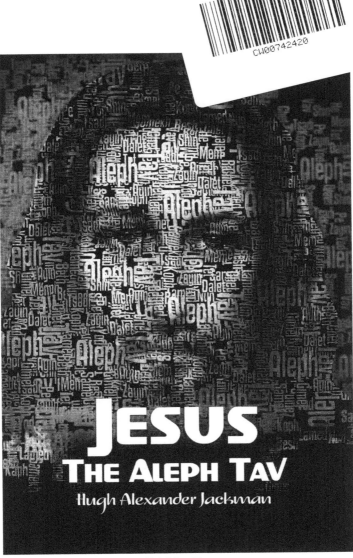

JESUS
THE ALEPH TAV
Hugh Alexander Jackman

Published by
Hugh Jackman Publishing
Cover Art adapted by Hugh Alexander Jackman
Based on an artist impression of
the Turin Shroud

JESUS THE ALEPH TAV

By Hugh A. Jackman DMin

© Hugh Alexander Jackman 2019

ISBN 978-0-9931358-6-6 Paperback

ISBN 978-0-9931358-7-3 e-book

ISBN 978-0-9931358-8-0 Audio Book

Published by Hugh Jackman Publishing

Websites
www.hughalexandermusic.com
www.spiritandlife.org.uk

The Aleph Tav

JESUS THE ALEPH TAV

FOREWORD
Gordon Pettie CEO Revelation TV

Some time ago, Hugh Jackman and his wife Seva were pre-senting a series of programmes on Revelation Television. The series was entitled Word and Prayer. Each week when they arrived at the studio, they came prepared to share with viewers, in the Word part of the programme, new truth they had learnt during the week from their study of the letters which make up the Hebrew alphabet. They dealt with a different letter each week.

It was quite clear that they could not wait to share what they had discovered during their research and study together, as to how each letter not only applied to the Scriptures, but pointed to the Lord Jesus Christ. Their excitement and enthusiasm to share was infectious and matched by viewers waiting to hear about the latest letter and the gems they had found.

The Bible describes our Holy Scriptures as manna from heaven. What Hugh and Seva were doing each week in their studies was allowing themselves to be directed by the Holy Spirit, into discovering fresh manna from the Scriptures, about the Hebrew language, and its relevance to our daily Christian walk. I am sure that you will find in this book material that it is likely you have not heard expounded elsewhere. It came across to me as fresh manna, as if from the Holy Spirit Himself.

Since the television programmes ended, Hugh has been doing further research into the subject and all the additional material is contained in this book.

So few Christians have had an opportunity of studying the Hebrew language. Many would love to but don't know where to begin. The Hebrew alphabet is made up of 22 characters. Most languages spoken in our world today are there for readers to learn by rote. Students will receive endless lists to memorise and verbs to conjugate. The Hebrew language is unique in its qualities. The 22 letters each paint a picture and point us back to the Scriptures.

I wonder how many of you have ever sat down and studied Psalm 119? It is the longest chapter in the entire Bible with 176 verses! Most of us know a few of the key verses in the Psalm. Verses such as: Open my eyes, that I may see wondrous things from your law (verse 18); and Your Word is a lamp to my feet and a light to my path (verse 105).

In this book Hugh has taken the 22 letters making up the Hebrew alphabet, with each one heading a portion of Psalm 119, and then by careful study, shown the harmony and synergy that comes from understanding the relationship between the letters and Christ. Be ready to learn new truths and become excited as you read this book.

When Hugh leads us in studying the fourth letter of the Hebrew language, Daleth, he links it to verses 25-32 of Psalm 119. He writes: When we pray intimately using the word of God, especially using these amazing Hebrew letters, three things immediately begin to happen.

Firstly, there is an AUTHENTICATION of the Power of the Word of God.

Secondly, there is a CONFIRMATION of the deity of the living Word. Christ.

Thirdly, and finally, there is a new fresh EXALTATION of the reality of His word in our hearts.

Wow. However old we are we have so much to learn. Get ready to study and open your heart to the Lord.

I have had the privilege to know Hugh and his wife Seva for many years now. I can vouch for their integrity and passion for our Lord and His Word - and it shows in this book.

Warmest greetings

Gordon Pettie

CEO, Revelation Television

JESUS THE ALEPH TAV

PREFACE
Jesus Christ Is the Hebrew Alphabet

As I was studying the word of God one day, I heard the voice of an old Kingdom general (now gone to be with the Lord) saying, "Every verse of Psalms 119 is a picture of the word of God."

His words gripped me. I could not get them out of my mind for the rest of that week. Eventually I sat down and quietly opened my Bible and began to read Psalm 119. Almost immediately the pictures began to jump out at me. It was a true word! But why had I not ever heard anyone preach about this?

I then noticed something just as significant. Every stanza (divided section) was chronologically arranged so that it was headed up with a Hebrew letter! Now this really got my attention. There are mysterious, and meaningful pictures hidden within the Hebrew letters just waiting to be discovered. I began to think, "Could it be that the words of this Psalm directly relate to each and every Hebrew letter?" I thought the Hebrew titles were placed there as a form of divider and organiser, much like the chapters and verses we have in our Bibles today. Our studies revealed the opposite to be true. The inspiration for each Psalm was given to its writers by divine inspiration of the Holy Spirit. This being true, then every Hebrew letter and its relevant stanza in Psalms 119 must form part of an ancient and largely unrecognised allegorical dictionary of the coming Messiah for the Jewish people, who of course is none other than our Christ and our Saviour. If you are part of the body of Christ, you know him as Jesus, the Christ, or the anointed one. If you are a Messianic Jew, you will know Him as Yeshua Ha Mashiac.

So how do we know that the letters point to the anointed Jesus? Let us begin our journey today, in John chapter 1.

"In the beginning was the Word, and the Word was with God, and the Word was God.
He was in the beginning with God. All things were made through Him, and without Him nothing was made that was made. In Him was life, and the life was the light of men. And the light shines in the darkness, and the darkness did not comprehend it". John 1:1-5

10

Look again at the words we just read. "In the beginning was the Word, and the Word was with God, and the Word was God". I recommend you repeat these words three times. Somehow this helps our finite minds to grasp what is being said.

"In the beginning was the Word, and the Word was with God, and the Word was God".
"In the beginning was the Word, and the Word was with God, and the Word was God".
"In the beginning was the Word, and the Word was with God, and the Word was God".

These Hebrew letters mean much more to us than I had first realised. They are as ancient as creation itself. They are an allegory of God's heart and His wonderful plan of salvation.

There are pictures of Christ and His earthly and heavenly mission in every single Hebrew letter and we are going to un -pack them and see them together in this devotional time. We will begin to see how Christ used these pictures in His own self biography. In other words, when He spoke, He used these wonderful allegories to describe the different facets of His own character.

I hope we can challenge you to make a diligent study of the

Hebrew Alphabet. Ask the Lord to open your mind and allow you to see the complete depths of it. I believe it will bring you closer to the Lord Jesus in every way possible. Just look at the way Jesus introduces Himself at the beginning of the book of Revelation

"I was in the Spirit on the Lord's Day, and I heard behind me a loud voice, as of a trumpet, saying, I am the Alpha and the Omega, the First and the Last". Revelation 1 : 10 & 11

The Lord Jesus Christ refers to Himself as the Alpha and Omega, (Greek letters occurring at the beginning and the end of the Greek alphabet). Of course we know that the first language of Christ was not English. Neither was it Greek for that matter. He spoke in an ancient form of Hebrew known as Aramaic. History also tells us that John the elder and revelator by that time also spoke and wrote Greek. Here is a revelation. Remember those tongues of fire?

"When the Day of Pentecost had fully come, they were all with one accord in one place. And suddenly there came a sound from heaven, as of a rushing mighty wind, and it filled the whole house where they were sitting. Then there appeared to them divided tongues, as of fire, and one sat upon each of them. And they were all filled with the Holy Spirit and began to speak with other tongues, as the Spirit gave them utterance". Acts 2:1-4

Note, they spoke with "other tongues" as the Spirit gave utterance. These were not strange sounds as referenced in the Biblical "unknown tongues". These were speaking other languages and dialects in the earth! The purpose being that the Gospel might be preached throughout the nations. We may therefore safely conclude that what Jesus actually said was

"I am the Aleph TAV"

John then translated this with his inspired knowledge of Greek. Aleph Tav is a Hebrew term which denotes the fullness of the covenant from God to man. It was a term that was added to the names of those founding fathers who were in covenant with God. They literally added these two letters to the end of their names as a sign of honour.

E.g. Abraham, the Aleph Tav Isaac, the Aleph Tav. Jacob, the Aleph Tav, Moses the Aleph Tav etc. Here is a big surprise for you. If you are in Christ, you can add your own name before the Aleph Tav - Hallelujah. What Jesus was actually saying was, "I am the Aleph Tav".

"I am also all of these things from Aleph through to Tav". The Hebrew Alphabet is not only history, it is **HIS STORY** and His gift from eternal God the Father to us.. Amen

Seva and I spent 6 months studying for this work. After the study, we sat together and wrote prayers for each letter. We wrote them exactly as they were revealed to us, literally exactly as they were laid on our hearts.

We thought about the many situations that we find ourselves in our daily lives, and through the Holy Spirit, found that these letters, like Jesus Christ Himself, the one which they were allegorising, seemed to cover our every need.

Before we go to the Alphabet, let me just add one more "beginning". We have seen the beginnings in both John and Revelation but let us not forget that the Bible itself begins with an absolutely stunning allegory of the Word of God. Let us go there together.

"In the beginning God created the heavens and the earth.
The earth was without form, and void;
and darkness was on the face of the deep.
And the Spirit of God was hovering over the face of the waters.
Then God said, "Let there be light"; and there was light".
Genesis 1:1 -2

The original Hebrew manuscripts, instead of 'Let there be light", put it this way:

LIGHT IN ME. . . BE.

The very first miracle that Father God does for us, is He creates LIGHT. How does He do this? He does it through His WORD. "Let there be LIGHT". He speaks His desire in the form of words and they instantly become reality!

Ladies and gentlemen, God had a vision of LIGHT. He formed that vision into a word and said "Let it be".

Those words travelled from the heart of God to His mouth and when they emerged, they were equipped with all of the power and purpose they needed to transform themselves into exactly what He had said. The very words themselves became LIGHT. May the words of this book be equipped with all of the power and purpose they need in order to be transformed into the very intentions for which they were created, in us.

Can you say Amen to that?

The other very important statement that I need to make is this: Ancient Hebrew was first a pictorial language. Each letter was first drawn rather than written. The shapes were later developed into a series of letters as we might know them today.

This devotional draws its conclusions firstly, from those original pictorial hieroglyphics, secondly, from historical canon, and thirdly (and most importantly) by the inspiration of the Holy Spirit.

We pray this book will be a total blessing to your life.

The first Letter

ALEPH

CHAPTER 1

ALEPH
The Sacrificial Oxen

"Blessed are the undefiled in the way,
Who walk in the law of the Lord!
Blessed are those who keep His testimonies,
Who seek Him with the whole heart! They also do no iniquity;
They walk in His ways.
You have commanded us To keep Your precepts diligently.
Oh, that my ways were directed to keep Your statutes!
Then I would not be ashamed,
When I look into all Your commandments.
I will praise You with uprightness of heart,
When I learn Your righteous judgments.
I will keep Your statutes;
Oh, do not forsake me utterly!"
Psalms 119 : 1-8

Aleph is the first Hebrew letter. Its stanza is found in Psalm 119:1-8. It is pictorially represented as the sacrificed oxen. It seems only right that the first letter should focus on the precious blood of sacrifice. Sacrificial blood holds a very sacred secret for us. However, before we can fully grasp what this means to us, let us closely examine what it would have meant to the Hebrew people. In Genesis chapter 4, Cain and Abel, sons of Adam and Eve, both brought offerings to the Lord.

"Now Abel was a keeper of sheep, but Cain was a tiller of the ground. And in the process of time it came to pass that Cain brought an offering of the fruit of the ground to the Lord. Abel also brought of the firstborn of his flock and of their fat. And the Lord respected Abel and his offering, but He did not respect Cain and his offering. And Cain was very angry, and his countenance fell". Genesis 4 : 1-5

There may be many reasons why Cain's offering was not respected by God. However, it is universally agreed that his libation was refused because it contained no shed blood in it. These were not like the days of perfection which his mother and father knew. Sin was now present in the earth. His offering therefore was a sin and guilt offering. His sin could not be atoned for without the shedding of blood. We find this out later in the book of Hebrews where we read:

"And according to the law almost all things are purified with blood, and without shedding of blood there is no remission".
Hebrews 9:22

You may be thinking but that was written thousands of years later, and that is true. However, God sees the end from the beginning so prophetically speaking, He could not accept a sacrifice for sin that did not contain shed blood.

Upon his dedication of the new temple which he had built, the Bible records King Solomon's efforts to ensure that his libation will be received, So we read in 2 Chronicles

"King Solomon offered a sacrifice of twenty-two thousand bulls and one hundred and twenty thousand sheep. So the king and all the people dedicated the house of God".
2 Chronicles 7: 5

In case you are thinking this is just a figure of speech, read the other accounts in both 1 Kings 8:64 and 2 Chronicles 7:7. Both bear references to the mammoth offering and the inability of the alter to contain the fat and blood from such a large liba-tion. Blood must have poured by the gallon as sacrifice after sacrifice were being brought before the High Priest. The Jews held a feast for seven full days whilst the sacrifices were being made. King Solomon's temple sacrifice is indeed significantly marked in scripture and history. It may well be the largest recorded libation in the Bible. As great as it was, I believe it serves only as a prophetic picture of an even greater offering that was to follow. This offering would be made not by many, but just one, yet the ramification of it will reverberate throughout eternity. I speak of the sacrifice made not by man, but by God Himself. The sacrifice of His only begotten son.

"Therefore, when He came into the world, He said: 'Sacrifice and offering You did not desire, But a body You have prepared for Me. In burnt offerings and sacrifices for sin You had no pleasure.' Then I said, 'Behold, I have come—In the volume of the book it is written of Me—To do Your will, O God. 'Previously saying, 'Sacrifice and offering, burnt offerings, and offerings for sin You did not desire, nor had pleasure in them' (which are offered according to the law), then He said, 'Behold, I have come to do Your will, O God.' He takes away the first that He may establish the second. By that will we have been sanctified through the offering of the body of Jesus Christ once for all". Hebrews 10:5-10

In this passage of scripture Jesus perfectly identifies Himself as the ultimate sacrifice. This is plain to see. However, can you also see that He is also confirming His story in the first letter of the Hebrew Alphabet. He is saying "I am Aleph!"

For us then, Aleph carries a very special picture. This picture speaks of the sacrificial blood of the Messiah, the precious blood of Christ. Some years ago I stood hands raised in a church in Harrow, London. I found myself taken in a vision to Holy Calvary where I was able to witness an awesome sight. I saw the upper part of a man's body nailed to a cross. I knew it was Jesus. I watched as the blood ran from his pierced hands or wrists right down into his armpits. I knelt and wept. That was the beginning of a time of deep and life-changing study for me.

Aleph brings us to our knees. It carries the essence of God's grace and mercy. It reminds us of His forgiveness and His love.

One of my favourite authors, Andrew Murray wrote the following words over 100 years ago:

"And now we also have liberty to enter through the Blood. Sin took away our liberty of approach to God, the Blood perfectly restores to us this liberty.
He who will take time to meditate upon the power of that Blood, appropriating it believingly for himself,
will obtain a wonderful view of the liberty and directness with which we can now have intercourse with God."
Andrew Murray, The Power of the Blood of Christ

So how does the writer of Psalms 119 connect Christ with this Aleph sacrifice? He opens with these words

"Blessed are the undefiled in the way" Psalm 119:1

Every human being on planet earth is born defiled by sin. This is without exception. There is only one way to become undefiled and that is through acceptance of the great messianic sacrifice. He also uses the term in the way. Jesus Christ said, "I am the way, the truth and the life". So only those in Christ may satisfy the condition. Simply put, accepting God's sacrificial offering, Jesus Christ, His son, The Word of God made flesh, makes you undefiled. Verse 3 says they do no iniquity. On the surface this phrase appears to be loaded with self-righteousness. As it appears to be making a boast of the believers own purity. On the other hand it could be saying that the believer inherits such a grace and power at conversion that the temptation to sin is completely eradicated! However, when we read this prophetically, the phrase paints a very different picture, one that we are quite familiar with.

'Whoever has been born of God does not sin, for His seed remains in him; and he cannot sin, because he has been born of God'. 1 John 3:9

However you read the words, it now seems clear that part of Messiah's mission was to implant His seed in us so that we would no longer be held under the bondage of sin. However you choose to understand it, we will all agree that the one who has accepted Messiah's perfect sacrifice is no longer able to sin.

We could spend some time debating as to the nature of the statement. However, for now it would suffice us to say that purity is achieved in Christ, either by grace or by conduct. This accords perfectly with the sentiment of the first stanza since all sacrifices were made for the purpose of atonement.

Authors note: With Aleph being the first letter, it is generally taken that the English equivalent will be A. However, please note that Aleph is one of two Hebrew letters with no equivalent sound. There is an equivalence chart at the back of this book in the glossary pages.

In conclusion, ALEPH represents the sacrificial animal. The first Hebrew letter takes us straight to the heart of God, directing us to Calvary and the shed blood of Jesus Christ by which we gain forgiveness and access to His great grace. Aleph rightly occupies first place in the Hebrew alphabet and our faith in Christ.

The Aleph Prayer

Lord we thank you for the supreme sacrifice which Christ made on the cross of Calvary. We acknowledge this sacrifice by accepting Jesus as the Lord and Saviour of our lives. Thank you for the amazing grace that comes to us through your suffering. You took the punishment for sin, so that we do not have to.

Thank you Lord. Amen.

The Second Letter

BETH

CHAPTER 2

BETH
The House (Dwelling Place)

How can a young man cleanse his way?
By taking heed according to Your word.
With my whole heart I have sought You;
Oh, let me not wander from Your commandments!
Your word I have hidden in my heart,
That I might not sin against You.
Blessed are You, O Lord! Teach me Your statutes.
With my lips I have declared All the judgments of Your mouth.
I have rejoiced in the way of Your testimonies,
As much as in all riches.
I will meditate on Your precepts, And contemplate Your ways.
I will delight myself in Your statutes; I will not forget Your word.

Psalms 119 verses 9-16

The second letter of the Hebrew alphabet is a most inter-esting one. It is derived from the hieroglyphic of a human dwelling place with a roof or a hut therefore today, Beth represents the house.

It is particularly interesting to the believer in Christ because we see clearly from scripture that Jesus referred to Himself many times as the very Beth or house that we should desire to dwell in. He also promised (in John 14:3) to prepare dwelling places for us in Heaven. Is this perhaps the main focus of Beth or is there something more hiding in this beautiful Hebrew letter? Let us begin with some amazing words from the Lord which accord perfectly with the letter Beth.

If you abide in Me, and My words abide in you. You will ask what you desire, and it shall be done for you. By this My Father is glorified, that you bear much fruit; so you will be My disciples.
John 15: 7-8

Here, the Lord's invitation is to "abide in me". Now when we break the word "abide" down it accords perfectly with the idea of a house or a dwelling place. He is saying I am inviting you to live in me. Now how are we as believers today going to be able to live in Christ?

As we study the Hebrew alphabet together we would like you to bear in mind that whilst WE need to be constantly reminded of the connection between Jesus and the Hebrew letters, He did not! A better way of saying that would be to say that Jesus Christ was always fully cognisant of the fact that He was, and is the living, walking, breathing, thinking, and speaking representation of the word of God in the flesh. And therefore in our lives.

When He says, 'I want you to live in me'. What He is actually saying is, "I am Beth and I want you to find my front door, use your key, open it up, walk inside and make yourself at home". He wants us to do that every day consistently. He wants us to live and abide in Him, always.

The obvious question for any new believer in Christ to ask would be: How do I do that? Where is the door? Where is the key? Is this a physical house I am supposed to find? Or, is He talking about that place He is preparing for us in Heaven? A spiritual mansion in the sky that we inherit after we die?

The answer is found in the remembrance of the fact that Jesus Christ is the word of God made flesh. This is the way that He describes Himself and it is the way that we need to constantly see Him. This is why Psalms 119 is so very important to the believer in Christ. It takes us to a place where we see Jesus Christ our Lord, the way He saw Himself. As the expressed vision of the living word of God.

An incredible thing occurs as we begin to unpack the Beth stanza with this knowledge. Returning to Psalms 119 verses 9 - 16. A doorway instantly opens which reveals the pathway to supernatural blessing and success for the believer. Note firstly, the five key phrases used within the verses. Your word, precepts, ways, judgements and statutes. All of these bear reference to the written or spoken word. Secondly, note the very first plea and response of the Psalm in verse 9.

"How can a young man cleanse his way? By taking heed according to your word" . Psalm 119 : 9

As we consider then the response to the question. This young man is admonished to take heed according to God's word.   Keeping closely in mind that these words are written under the covering of Beth, the house.   We learn therefore, that God does not just want us to take heed of the word on one occasion but that He wants us to abide in the word permanently.   This isn't about reading, studying and remembering. This is about being at the place where we are living daily under His precepts and His Word. Note again in verse 11

"Your word I have hidden in my heart that I might not sin against you"

When something is hidden in your heart it means that even when you're not thinking about a matter, it remains present there. You may not be focused upon it, yet it is never too far away, just bubbling under the surface, shaping your direction and your thoughts. When the word of God surreptitiously develops more authority than your own natural thinking, you are living in the word of God and therefore you are abiding in Christ. It is therefore a state of constant awareness of God. Never forgetting. A state where your spirit is delighting itself in His awesome presence.

Do you not know that you are the temple of God and that the spirit of God dwells in you? Corinthians 3:16

Corinthians now teaches us about the special name of the house where God lives. This is called a temple. Since we are now the bona fide dwelling place of God, the Spirit of God finds also a most suitable place to dwell. In you! Whilst the Psalmist could not yet speak much of this (for Christ had not yet ascended to the cross of Calvary). This is where the believer in Christ enjoys a very special privilege.

It is through the indwelling presence of the Holy Spirit that we are ultimately enjoined to God. Through this union, we find and enjoy fellowship, favour, communication, love and guidance. As we live in Him and He in us, the wondrous fruit of that relationship is born. This stanza also brings us, throughout its verses, a special sense of the preciousness of the word of God. Many years ago whilst living in the UK, I bought a metal detector. This device has followed me all around the world but I have never actually used it! Though it lives in the back of my car. It seems that I enjoy the idea of metal detecting for treasure far more than the actual process. I will get around to doing some detecting one day. I love the idea that you could just go out in a field and find hidden treasure!

The testimonies of God, according to verse 14, are to be rejoiced in as much as riches. Jesus Christ described The Kingdom of God as being like the man who found a pearl of great price in a field and buried it again after purchasing the field. The word of God really is precious. It is honourable and holy. It should always be treated as such. It is far more valuable than any treasure you could find. That really excites me because one never knows what the day may bring us from spending time in the word of God.

"Do not lay up for yourselves treasures on earth, where moth and rust destroy and where thieves break in and steal; but lay

up for yourselves treasures in heaven, where neither moth nor rust destroys and where thieves do not break in and steal. For where your treasure is, there your heart will be also".
Matthew 6: 19 -21

Verse 14 could be translated this way. 'Prophetically speaking, the word of God that we meditate on today, will become our state of being tomorrow'. It will form our house. In other words, we will live in today, that which we meditated upon yesterday. That is why we should treasure the Word of God. It is the thermostat which sets the temperature of our tomorrow.

In Closing Beth, let us return to verse 10 at the beginning of this section.

"Oh let me not wander from your commandments"!

My friends let us take heed of these most sobering words. Wander seems to convey a sense of walking aimlessly. Perhaps without thinking. In plain English, beware of distractions as we walk out our lives in Christ. May God help us to stay aware of the fact that we are dwelling in Him through Jesus Christ. Much like our conscious would remind us that it is not pertinent to kick a football around in our front room or to burn a camp fire in bed. Some things belong inside the house and other things do not. As we walk out our lives in Christ may we be aware of worldly outside influences which will try to infiltrate our dwelling place. Rather than the works of the flesh, may we be filled with the fruit of the Spirit. I am sure that as you meditate on this letter, God will further personalise it for you. With this foundation laid I am sure God will take you to deeper depths of revelation through the word.

Our purpose is to plant the seed and give it some water but only God can make it grow.

In conclusion, Beth represents the House. It reminds us that Christ not only provides a dwelling place for us in God after we leave earth, but also that He is our dwelling place and that He dwells in us who are born again. Indeed in Him we live and move and have our being. (Acts 17:28)

Beth is a two way revelation.
We are the House He lives in
And He is the House we live in

Beth

Jesus the Aleph Tav

BETH TESTIMONY

The following is an excerpt from another book I have written called Facts vs. Truth. I have decided to include it because it reveals a personal testimony in connection with the letter Beth. It perfectly illustrates how important the revelation of the House (God's indwelling Presence) really is.

The word of God is Truth that can overcome any fact. The following is an accurate record of a healing which I received by the Holy Spirit. I have shared it all over the world and it carries the anointing presence every time I do. I have been blessed to receive all manner of healings through the Lord's anointed presence in my life. They were all glorious at the time. However, this particular healing left a powerful and indelible mark on me forever.

In 2006 my wife and I launched a television ministry. This was a huge step of faith which took a lot out of me financially and inevitably physically. As the pressure of the ministry mounted, I began to feel the effects of that pressure on my body. It began with a strange tiredness which I could not shake off. A year after launching the channel I had to close the whole thing down. We suffered major financial loss and I ended up spending weeks in bed wondering what had happened to me. The tiredness just got progressively worse until eventually, I began to suffer with a form of **Chronic Fatigue Syndrome**, a condition that results from a number of ailments, most of them are serious. I prayed every day and received some relief but ultimately the condition only seemed to worsen. I visited the doctor and described my symptoms, which by now had increased in both number and severity. I had debilitating pain in different parts of my body. A consistent horrible nausea, which was accompanied by that awful tiredness. The best way I can describe it is that it felt as though I was close to death. I was feeling desperate. Finally, I began to give more careful attention to God's Word, the Holy Bible. I remembered the scripture, which said that His Word was health and healing to my flesh.

For they are life to those who find them, And health to all their flesh. Proverbs 4:22

I began to read from the pen of one of my favourite authors who is now in Heaven. His name was Charles Capps. The book was called Faith and Confession.

The Word of God through Mr. Capps began to transform my thinking. I understood that healing could be mine through the confession of the Word of God by faith.

Faith began to grow and I began to believe that I could be healed from these dastardly symptoms.

All I had to do is find the right words to confess from the Word of God. It sounded so simple but it was just the beginning of the battle. I do not remember which part of the book did it. Mr Capps's words were like ballistic missiles striking at unbelief and poor teaching. Every sentence seemed to knock down old sacred cows. My faith was growing, precept upon precept and line upon line.

As I studied His Word, I began to feel somewhat better but a battle began to ensue. It seemed that I would feel better for a short time but then the sickness would return with a vengeance, this time more painfully and with much more debilitating effect. Many times I would be reduced to tears. All I could do was beg and plead with God through my tears. Even with all of my studying and prayers, I still was not getting the point.

After some weeks, I was hit with the worst attack ever. I feared for my life as the tiredness seemed to be increasing. I was so tired that I could not even get to sleep! I thought to myself, if this is how life had to be, I would be better off dead.

One evening, I was laid on my front room floor because I did not have the strength to do anything else. I thought to myself, I do not think I can carry on anymore. I fought the battle and lost. A real deep and penetrating fear suddenly came over me. I was so tired that I truly feared that I would die from this thing. I have always been quite an emotional person, and I thought to myself I better get upstairs to the bedroom where my wife was sleeping. After all, if I am going to die, at least let me be with some-one I love and who loves me.

I was so battle weary, I was ready to give up the ghost in defeat, but as I crawled up the stairs of our home, I heard the Lord speaking inside of me. He said, "You shall not die, but LIVE". I was a pitiful sight by this time, a grown man, quietly weeping on the floor of my bedroom beside my bed because I did not have the strength to get into it. My wife Seva was in bed but she was not sleeping. She was reading her Bible. She held out her hand to me and began to pray quietly. I did not want her to know how ill I was feeling and at the same time, somewhere in the back of my mind I remembered what the Lord had said. You shall not DIE but LIVE! I said I am sorry Hon. (I was always saying these words because I was living in a state of continual sorrow) I said to her, that if I could just find the right Words to pray, I am sure I will be healed but I just do not know what to pray or say. She held out her hand to me and I took hold of it. As I held her hand, instead of confessing what the Word of God says, I spoke out what I felt. I said "I just do not have any strength". At that moment, this was a FACT. I could not deny it anymore because I did not seem to have any strength.

Seva, now half asleep, paused for a moment and then spoke the following words to me:

"The Lord is your strength and your shield".

I heard the words. I thought about what she had said. At first my mind dismissed it as Christianeese. (In case you have never heard that phrase before, it refers to stuff that people say that comes from a Christian religious source but not necessarily scripture based or from the heart). Then I thought that's a scripture isn't it? I replied, what did you say? She repeated the words

"The Lord is your strength and your shield"...

Now I was vaguely familiar with these words. I had heard them in a song or read them in a psalm I thought. Deep down I knew they were scriptural, but they meant nothing more to me other than being a source of distant but non relevant encouragement. I said what chapter and verse was that in the Bible? As I laid on the floor Seva began to thumb her way through her old leather Bible which she kept by her bedside. "I found it! She said,

Psalms 28:7 ". The Lord is my strength and shield".

The room was completely silent after that but thunder began to rumble on the inside of me. What did I just hear? How can this be?

Have you ever received a word from God that completely and utterly belies your situation? Well that day I did. I heard life in those words. Hallelujah! I heard my ticket to freedom from this evil disease that I was being gripped by.

I said, The Lord is My Strength, The Lord is My Strength, The Lord is My Strength, The Lord is My Strength! As I spoke these words, my mind seemed to argue with me. If the Lord is your strength, why are you so weak? A war literally broke out within me! It was a battle between my Spirit and My Mind!

Then a thought came from deep within me. It was the voice of God! He said, I am in you, through the Anointing. You see I had spent my first 10 years of Christianity pretty much studying the Word Christ. I was completely fascinated with it and when I started preaching I only had the one message and I preached it everywhere I went. Christ the Anointed One and His Anointing. Well, I did not realise it back then but the years of studying the anointing were about to suddenly and miraculously produce incredible fruit in my life. You see,

I KNEW as a certain TRUTH that the Lord had made His dwelling in me through CHRIST - Hallelujah

I knew that God, through His Holy Word would be incapable of lying to me. (Authors note: I knew nothing about the letter Beth or the relevance of Psalm 119 at that time but I had a perfect knowledge of God's indwelling in my house). When my wife said the Lord is your strength, there was an undeniable connection made between my spirit and my mind.

Finally, I repeated the following deduction. The Lord is in me and the Lord is my strength, the Lord is in me and the Lord is my strength. Finally, The following words just popped out of my mouth. I just felt as if there was an earthquake in my stomach and I was about to erupt. They just exploded from the deepest part of my being.

"If the Lord is my Strength and the Lord lives in me, then I have all of the strength I need".

At that moment I realised that I had been crying deep inside for more than three months. The tears may not have been falling at that moment but I was feeling so sorry for myself, the grief alone was enough to kill me. I instantly stopped crying inside and started speaking the following words out loud "The Lord is in me, His strength is in me"! The more I spoke it, the happier I got. It was as if my spirit had been stooped over waiting for my inevitable demise but something had changed on the inside. My friends, I gradually made my way from the floor, to one leg. Finally, I raised my head up and declared with a smile "I am healed!" Immediately, before I knew what had happened to me, I was standing, leaping and running around the room, Hallelujah! I had been healed by the presence of God in me. I never suffered that sickness again as I have been walking in the strength of the Lord ever since that night.

Whenever I would feel that tiredness trying to come back it would be whipped into place by the Word of God. Glory to God! The almighty Word of His Power delivered me and continues to do so today. There were a number of factors working together that got me that healing but now, more than ten years later I finally began to understand what happened.

The fact was, I had no strength BUT the Truth is according to Psalms 28:7 The Lord IS my strength. Understanding that God's Word is TRUTH produces miracles!

If you are seeking a healing from God, start confessing the following words daily, hourly or even every ten minutes. God's Word is TRUTH. No matter what the symptoms say. Those symptoms are your mountain. They will be moved by the greater truth of God's Word. Jesus said if you believe that you have what you say, you will have what you say. I say you are healed in Jesus name.

Now you know the truth! Do not sit in silence! If you are truly in need of healing, I implore you today, trust the Lord. Trust His Word. How? Find out what God's word says about your condition. Do not trust the symptoms, trust in the TRUTH! Find the scriptures that pertain to your case.

Read them over and over. Keep reading and confessing them until they become your personal reality. Keep telling yourself what the Bible says. Remember, there is life in the Word of God and healing for your body.

Do not worry if you do not understand it with your mind. Your heart knows how to extract that life. It was created for that very purpose. You are what you eat! So just keep feeding your heart (the true centre of your being) with the truth from God's Word.

Confession

I thank you heavenly Father, that you have made every provision for my healing through your written word. I confess that your word is the truth. I confess there is life in your word. Your word is the final authority in my life. Even if the facts say otherwise, I will confess the word of God. Your word is the truth that can change any fact. My symptoms are nothing more than the testimony of the sense realm but I confess your Word.

End of Testimony - Authors note.

Yes my friends, Jesus is the word of God which became flesh and dwelt among us. He is the House we live in. We are the House He dwells in. Those that will meditate upon and appropriate this fully will without doubt receive credible blessings from His divine presence. I can present no greater proof of the miracle of His indwelling presence than this wonderful testimony of His grace. I pray your faith will be encouraged by it.

The Beth Prayer

Dear Lord, you said in John 15:4 that we should abide in you and you would abide in us. Help us to stay focussed on your word. We thank you that these words are true and we thank you for your abiding presence in our lives. No matter what circumstances befall us, we know that we can always abide in your presence through you and through your word.

Amen

The Third Letter

GIMEL

CHAPTER 3

GIMEL
The Camel (Burden Bearer)

*Deal bountifully with Your servant,
That I may live and keep Your word. Open my eyes,
that I may see
Wondrous things from Your law.
I am a stranger in the earth;
Do not hide Your commandments from me.
My soul breaks with longing For Your judgments at all
times. You rebuke the proud the cursed, Who stray
from Your commandments.
Remove from me reproach and contempt,
For I have kept Your testimonies.
Princes also sit and speak against me,
But Your servant meditates on Your statutes.
Your testimonies also are my delight And my counselors.
Psalms 119 : 17-24*

What a beautiful picture is painted for us by the third letter in the Hebrew Aleph Tav (Alphabet). Gimel was once hieroglyphically represented as a camel.

The Hebrew root word is Gamel. This is a word that means to wean like a child. This letter consequently presents to us two perfect and beautiful allegories. Firstly, we see the camel. This animal is an extraordinary burden bearer. Used primarily in hot, arid climates because they can travel long distances in extreme heat. They are able to store water, fat and other nutrients in their humps. Secondly, Gamel depicts a child weaner. Every child must reach a stage where he or she must learn to chew properly. Moving from mothers milk on to solid food. This process is known as weaning.

Let us look firstly at the camel and its ability to carry water. How is this a picture of Christ? Jesus Christ came to earth in the driest season that Israel had ever known. Spiritually speaking, there was a drought. There were no miracles taking place. There were no extraordinary healings or deliverances. The Jews were, in a sense, in captivity to the Romans. It had seemed as if the glory days of Joshua and David had long since past.

This was a dry and arid season for the Jewish people and then suddenly Isaiah's prophecy from the 53rd chapter and verse 2 seemed to come alive. He was indeed like a root out of dry ground. Consider the words of Christ to the Samaritan woman at the well.

"Whoever drinks of this water will thirst again, but whoever drinks of the water that I shall give him will never thirst. But the water that I shall give him will become in him a fountain of water springing up into everlasting life." John 4 : 13 - 14

Christ came full of anointing, loaded with streams of blessing. He had rivers of living water stored in His prophetical humps. Enough to bring every one of us through the dry and torrid deserts of our lives. He came ready to wash us in the water of the word and to baptise us in the river of His blessing.

Yes! Christ associates Himself with Gimel. You can see it clearly in the case of this woman. In fact, I dont think you will ever see a camel the same way again. His amazing outstretched neck speaks of his ability to reach places no other can reach. While He was on earth Christ reached to the heavens and now in the heavens He reaches back to earth to save us. He remembers that we are strangers in the earth, in it but not of it. (John 15:18)

The second picture the camel paints for us comes from its root 'Gamal', which as I stated earlier, means to wean like a child. This is the understanding with which the Psalmist appears to be writing. His opening request is for God to deal bountifully with him. The English translation of the word bountiful means to be liberal or generous in bestowing gifts or favours. The direct Hebrew translation however is simply the word Gamal! We can take this to mean that God's purpose for weaning us is to bring us to His generosity. To bring us to His divine favour and to bless us abundantly.   Hallelujah!

Jesus Christ spoke of the need to become like children in order to enter the Kingdom of Heaven. Again, this is another reference to the weaning process that we must all undergo as believers.

Peter reminds us that during this period of weaning He is our great burden bearer. I have wonderful memories of those first days as a born-again believer in Jesus Christ. How He did so many things for me. He took away my burdens and opened my eyes to see wondrous things. I had nothing to worry about except to be devoted to the study of His word. I rolled all of my cares and burdens over to Him.

Casting all your care upon Him, for He cares for you.
1 Peter 5:7

Jesus the Aleph Tav

I can still hear the beat of the tambourines in unison as we sang that wonderful chorus.

Cast your burdens onto Jesus for He cares for you, higher higher higher higher higher higher higher higher lift Jesus higher

I wonder if those Pentecostal's of old knew what they were writing when they penned these words. Yes my friends as we study these beautiful Hebrew letters together, it is evident that Gimel can only point to one person. The Lord Jesus Christ and no other.

In conclusion, Gimel represents the Camel. It primarily represents a picture of the way in which we grow through the living Word of God. Gimel also demonstrates the way Christ carries our heaviest burdens as He sets us free from the load of sin. Through this process of load bearing, He brings us to the place of being weaned in His goodness and grace.

The Gimel Prayer

Lord, there are times in our lives when we do not have the strength to carry our own burdens. It is in these moments of human weakness that we learn to rely on you to take our problems and situations on as your own. We trust you to do this now, as we hand you our heavy burdens that we cannot carry, in Jesus name. For this we thank you. And for those who do not know your lovingkindness, we pray that you will be their burden bearer also.

The Fourth letter

DALETH

CHAPTER 4

DALETH
The Door or Gate

My soul clings to the dust;
Revive me according to Your word.
I have declared my ways, and You answered me;
Teach me Your statutes. Make me understand the way of Your
precepts; So shall I meditate on Your wonderful works.
My soul melts from heaviness;
Strengthen me according to Your word.
Remove from me the way of lying,
And grant me Your law graciously.
I have chosen the way of truth; Your judgments I have laid
before me. I cling to Your testimonies;
O Lord, do not put me to shame!
I will run the course of Your commandments,
For You shall enlarge my heart.
Psalms 119: 25-32

When we pray intimately using the word of God, especially using these amazing Hebrew letters, three things immediately begin to happen. Firstly, there is an AUTHENTICATION of the Power of the Word of God. Secondly, there is a CONFIRMATION of the deity of the living Word. Christ. Thirdly, and finally, there is a new fresh EXALTATION of the reality of His word in our hearts. I believe this letter will transform our thinking and in a real sense, clear the way to understanding the rest of the Aleph Tav (Alphabet). By now I am sure you will understand the format of this teaching so you will know that Daleth was originally hieroglyphically drawn as a door. Daleth therefore represents a door or a gate. Bible scholars among you will immediately start to recall the scriptures where Jesus referred to Himself in this way. This is absolutely crystal clear evidence of the fact that Christ knew exactly who He was when He walked the earth. Let us begin with two very well read verses.

Then Jesus said to them again, "Most assuredly, I say to you, I am the door of the sheep. All who ever came before Me are thieves and robbers, but the sheep did not hear them. I am the door. If anyone enters by Me, he will be saved, and will go in and out and find pasture".
John 10 : 7-8

"Behold, I stand at the door and knock. If anyone hears My voice and opens the door, I will come in to him and dine with

him, and he with Me". Revelation 3:20

We are going to break this section down into three main thoughts. We will trust the Holy Spirit to do the rest.
   We are going to talk about the following three doors. The door of love, the door of access and the door of decision.

The first door is the door of love.

Both of these two scriptures demonstrate the love of God towards us. They also teach us something else about doors. They can swing in both directions, both towards us and away from us. The first opens to God through Jesus but the second swings towards us from the Father. He sends His love to us but does not force us to receive it. Rather He stands outside and gently knocks at the door of our hearts.
The scripture lets us know that it is up to us to respond to His approach by opening the door. God is a gentle God. Consequently, He will not enter without our invitation.

"I am the way, the truth, and the life. No one comes to the Father except through Me." Matthew 14: 6B

In the book of Exodus, God commanded Moses to build a tabernacle in the wilderness. It was like a movable tent of worship. He was given explicit instructions for its building and layout. The entrance of the main thoroughfare was guarded by a door. This is commonly referred to as the gate of the tabernacle. This gate was the only way to approach the Father from earth in those days. Can you see the connection?

Please remember that Jesus and His disciples did not have the New Testament as we know it today. Their Bible was the Talmud (Torah) a collection of scrolls which we know today as the Old Testament. Through His great love, God made a way of access for the people of Israel to approach Him. There was no other way. In the same way, God's love has provided a way for us to access Him today. That way is Jesus Christ. He is the Daleth to God. This door will remain open until the fullness of the Gentiles has come in. Dear friend, do you feel as if you can sense the Lord knocking at your heart door right now? If you do, and want to respond, you will find a special prayer at the end of this chapter which has brought millions to Christ before you.

The second door is the door of access:

When we looked at the letter Beth we saw that the Lord invited us to abide in Him and allow His word to abide in us. He said we would ask what we will and it would be done for us. Through this scripture we understand that the word of God is also a Daleth.

God has provided everything we need through His word. He has made provision for our sickness, poverty, anxieties, mental anguishes and grief. The door swings towards us saying yes and amen to all who will make a request by faith.

Note: The believer must ask using words emanating from His abiding presence. Not only is He the gate that allows access, He is also the provision that we need.

> *"You search the Scriptures, for in them you think you have eternal life; and these are they which testify of Me."*
> *John 5:39.*

Jesus is the way the truth and the life. His presence within us produces all we need in order to activate all of Heaven's provision for us here on earth. Hallelujah.!

The third door is the door of decision

This is the door that we have total control over. It is the door of choice. God has done all that He can to get His provision to us. Whether we receive that provision or not is entirely up to us. This is why we study the Scriptures. To know and understand more about Jesus. The Bible declares that faith comes by hearing and hearing by the word. The more we hear and comprehend about Jesus, the more our faith will grow. Facts diminish as they are replaced by divine truths. Power and faith overcome our weaknesses. Light triumphs over darkness, and good over evil if only we will trust God, open the door and say yes. Provision is waiting on the other side.

The Psalmist clearly understands our struggle between the flesh and the spirit. He opens this stanza with the words

"My soul clings to the dust; Revive me according to Your word."

What does he mean by the words my soul clings to the dust? God is a triune being. We likewise, having been made in His image are likewise triune. We are Spirits! We possess a soul (Essentially mind) and live in a body. When God's presence or anointing comes into our lives a struggle often ensues. This is the struggle the Psalmist is speaking about. He feels a natural drawing (through his flesh) to death. He is saying open the door to life that I may live. His cry is "revive me according to your word".

The Bible has much more to teach us on this subject. As we follow Christ to the book of John chapter 9, where we see the

Lord passing by a man who was blind from birth. At this point, His disciples ask Him a question. "Rabbi, who sinned, this man or his parents, that he was born blind"? Now, if you analyse this carefully you will find that this was a loaded question. For how could the man have sinned before he was born? Note the Lord's answer.

"Neither this man, nor his parents sinned, but that the works of God be made manifest in him". John 9: 3

What did Jesus mean by the words "The works of God"? I believe He was referring to God's perfect plan of salvation for mankind, which He was about to demonstrate through the healing of this very blind man.

"As long as I am in the world, I am the light of the world". When He had thus spoken, He spat on the ground, and made clay of the spittle, and he anointed the eyes of the blind man with the clay, And said unto him, Go, wash in the pool of Siloam, (which is by interpretation, Sent.) He went his way therefore, and washed, and came seeing John 9: 5-7

What was the Lord doing? He literally spat His saliva on the ground! Can you picture Him making putty in His hands by stirring the spittle and the dust together. Let us now put our scientific hats on for a moment and talk a little about DNA. The definition is quite long winded so I shortened it.

A nucleic acid that carries the genetic information in the cell and is capable of self- replication and synthesis of RNA. In simple terms, DNA carries the entire physical formula of the creature from which it came.

Forensic science today needs only a small sample of a person's saliva to determine the DNA characteristics of the human being from which the sample came. In other words, the complete molecular pattern of the entire man is contained in his saliva. People today are convicted and sent to prison based on DNA evidence alone.

According to the book of Genesis, God made man from the dust of the ground. We can conclude therefore that the DNA of the son of God (the perfect, sinless and incorrupt) Jesus Christ is being mixed with the dust from which God created Adam the one who fell into sin (This is who we were before salvation). I hope you can see it, the perfect DNA of God is being combined with the corrupt flesh of man. As Jesus anoints the eyes of the blind man, a credible miracle takes place. When Jesus anointed him with His DNA, the blindness disappeared. People who had watched him beg daily for years simply could not recognise him anymore. Likewise, when Jesus comes into our lives, He is the door to total change in every possible way.

In conclusion Daleth clearly points to the Lord Jesus Christ because He is the only way to the Father and therefore the only way to receive His love and His word . It also reminds us that salvation must begin with a personal decision to let Jesus the Messiah (The Christ) in. Finally Daleth reminds us that we were born in corrupted Adamic flesh with our bodies on a sure course for death from the very day that we were born. But we have Jesus Christ the Aleph Tav. He is the Daleth that opens to us bringing the life of God not just into our spirit and soul but also into our physical bodies that we might live and not die.

Hallelujah.

The Daleth Prayer

*Heaven Father, You have knocked. I am answering now.
I believe in Jesus Christ and acknowlede Him in my life today. I
receive you as my Lord and saviour and ask you to forgive all of
my sin. From this day forward please receive me as your son. I
thank you Lord that you have opened the door and that now
Heaven's gates of blessing, healing, prosperity, life and love are
available to me. Thank you for the truth that the way is now
open for the Holy Spirit and angelic intervention in my life.
Most of all I thank you for the ever present river of the grace of
salvation flowing towards us through your son
Jesus Christ.*

Amen

The Fifth Letter

HE

Jesus the Aleph Tav

CHAPTER 5

HE
The Lattice Window

Teach me, O Lord, the way of Your statutes,
And I shall keep it to the end. Give me understanding, and I
shall keep Your law; Indeed, I shall observe it with my whole
heart. Make me walk in the path of Your commandments,
For I delight in it. Incline my heart to Your testimonies,
And not to covetousness.
Turn away my eyes from looking at worthless things,
And revive me in Your way.
Establish Your word to Your servant,
Who is devoted to fearing You. Turn away my reproach which I
dread, For Your judgments are good.
Behold, I long for Your precepts;
Revive me in Your righteousness.
Psalms 119: 33-40

The letter 'He' represents the lattice window. The Jewish people believe that this letter holds a particular prophetic message for all of mankind. As you look at He, it is meant to give you the sense of a lattice window that is always open. Somewhat like a venetian blind that is left open so that the sun can always come through but yet people cannot see from the outside. The idea is that the Lord God is always open to receive man if he makes his approach the right way. Remember again that Jesus Christ is the word made flesh. It is through Christ that we have this open window.

Incredibly, this tiny letter He, forms two constituent parts of the true name of God! Let us break that down. The names Yahweh and Jehovah are both derived from hidden Jewish meanings. The Hebrews hallowed the name of God to the point that they would not ever say or write His name. We do know however, that the name was formed from three Hebrew letters and you will notice that "He" is used twice. Here are the elements of the name:

Yod - He - Vav - He

We will revisit this name later in our study after we have studied the letters Yod and Vav. However, please notice that the open window occurs twice. Is this a possible reference to the Lord's return? Two windows of opportunity for mankind?

" For I do not desire, brethren, that you should be ignorant of this mystery, lest you should be wise in your own opinion, that blindness in part has happened to Israel until the fullness of the Gentiles has come in. And so all Israel will be saved, as it is written".
Romans 11:25 - 26 (a)

The key word in this scripture seems very insignificant and can easily be missed. Please note the word "until" used here

"Until" the fullness of the Gentiles has come in.

This tiny word lets us know something incredible. Prophetically speaking, there will come a day when in God's judgement the last Gentile will be saved. The fullness will come in. This moment will trigger a series of prophetically predicted events which will usher mankind into the last of the last days. Grace will still abound for mankind even after these days in the darkest times of the book. Revelation predicts that God will still keep that window open. He will still allow people to be saved right up until the very final trumpet sounds.

Consider this. What is the purpose of a window? It is to allow light and fresh air to enter the house. There is a beautiful connection between the window and the light which will become abundantly clear when we reach verse 130 of Psalm 119. (If you are anything like me you will probably want to cheat and jump ahead and study the letter Pe now.) Essentially this is a *derash* revelation, meaning there is a bridge between the two separate statements that makes them one.

The entrance of your word brings light. Psalms 119:130

Here is the bridge. The letter "Pe" referenced by verses 129-136, is symbolic of the mouth. The mouth is the instrument from which words come forth. Jesus is the word. He is also the light of the world. Ladies and gentlemen, allow me to repeat something I said in the introduction of this book. The very first miracle that Father God does for us, is He creates LIGHT. How does He do this? He does it through His WORD.

"Let there be LIGHT".

He speaks His desire in the form of words and they instantly become reality!

God had a vision of LIGHT. He formed that vision into a word and said "Let it be". Those words travelled from the heart of God to His mouth and when they emerged, they were equipped with all of the power and purpose they needed to transform themselves into exactly what He had said. The very words themselves became LIGHT. Can you see the bridge? Light is made of the word. If man was fully able to break light down to its constituent elements, you will find at its core, the word. The modern science of string theory attests to this theoretically.

The Psalmist presents for us in this stanza, his interpretation of light which, transliterated, would be closer to the term 'enlightenment'. The sense that to understand something fully is to be enlightened. This is evidenced by his requests throughout the section. Teach me, and give me understanding is his heart cry. King David clearly understood that God was not only the source for life, but also for divine wisdom and understanding. Amen!

In conclusion 'He' , represents the lattice window. Twice mentioned in the name Yahweh. 'He' reminds us that He (God) has provided a way and a time for us to see His grace and provision and that the light of God enters in ONLY through His Word. (Jesus Christ, The Messiah)

The He Prayer

Heavenly Father, we thank you for your awesome, powerful, life changing, unchangeable word which empowers us by faith as we trust in, rely on and depend on it. Today we declare that our lives are established by and through your word and the presence of the Lord Jesus Christ through the Holy Spirit. We pray that our loved ones will see the light whist it is still day.

Amen

The Sixth Letter

WAW

Jesus the Aleph Tav

CHAPTER 5

WAW
The Hook

Let Your mercies come also to me, O Lord
Your salvation according to Your word.
So shall I have an answer for him who reproaches me,
For I trust in Your word.
And take not the word of truth utterly out of my mouth,
For I have hoped in Your ordinances.
So shall I keep Your law continually,
Forever and ever. And I will walk at liberty,
For I seek Your precepts.
I will speak of Your testimonies also before kings,
And will not be ashamed.
And I will delight myself in Your commandments, Which I love.
My hands also I will lift up to Your commandments,
Which I love, And I will meditate on Your statutes.
Psalms 119 : 41-48

Our fantastic journey now brings us to the amazing letter Waw, which represents a hook or a peg.

Generally speaking, hooks are very practical. They are widely used in our own lives today. We hang our clothes, kitchen utensils, bathroom towels, and garden tools on hooks. Song writers call a great chorus the hook. Fishermen feed the world with hooks. Think of your world without any hooks.

The importance of this Hebrew letter is immediately apparent as it is the third constituent part of the Hebrew name for God

Yod He WAW He (Yahweh)

This is further confirmed with Yahweh's instruction to Moses to build the tabernacle. The moveable tent of worship that will house the presence of God in the earth. The Waw or pegs are the small but ingenious element of the construction which literally fastened and held the entire structure together. The white linen, the veil of the temple, the badger skins. Everything about the structure depended upon the stability of the hooks. Our study of waw was particularly fascinating for us because likewise it seemed to be describing that facet of Christ's identity that literally holds our faith together. Our definition of waw is therefore as follows.

Waw teaches us that the word of God (Jesus) is the "living thing" that you can hang your faith on.

Gods laws, His promises, His ordinances and His counsel are the things that hold the structure of this world together. Without them, the entire earth has no solidarity and will fail. Prophetically speaking, this is exactly where our world is heading right now. The removal of God's underpinning strength leaves this world open to the destructive forces of the enemy.

Yes, the word of God is the ONLY living thing that you can hang your faith on. I have received many miracles from the Lord. There were miracles of provision, finance, jobs, protection etc. Most significantly, I have enjoyed several healings directly from the hand of God. The miracles themselves, became things that I could hang my faith on in the future. Likewise when I would share with others about what God had done. These miracles became things that others could hang their faith on.

Consequently, in Waw, we see a picture of the word being multiplied as it is magnified, moving from one heart to another!

Testimonies alone cannot uphold the truths associated with waw so let us add evidence from scripture to support this claim, beginning in the book of Hebrews.

"Who being the brightness of His glory and the express image of His person, and upholding all things by the word of His power, when He had by Himself purged our sins, sat down at the right hand of the Majesty on high", Hebrews 1 : 3

Pay close attention to the words 'Upholding all things by the word of His power'. Note: ALL things! Also do not overlook the significant twist that the scripture gives us. We would have expected it to read 'the power of His word'. However, the Holy Spirit's intention here is to show that the word is the source of the power and not the reverse. Hence "The word of His Power!". The more you meditate on this, the more you will really begin to see why it was writ-ten this way. Anyone may speak powerful words but only God and His children can speak words which are power! Hallelujah!

He is the image of the invisible God, the firstborn over all creation. For by Him all things were created that are in heaven and that are on earth, visible and invisible, whether thrones or dominions or principalities or powers. All things were created through Him and for Him. And He is before all things, and in

Him all things consist. Colossians 1 : 15-17
Amplified Verse 17 *And He Himself existed before all things,
and in Him all things consist (cohere, are held together).*

The scriptures clearly show that all things are held together by the word of God. Waw's prophetic message to us, is a mighty one indeed. It is teaching us that the word of God is the centre and substance of our faith. Faith without the word of God is merely natural human faith. It is impossible to have the God kind of faith without the God kind of word. I remember reading the 11th chapter of Hebrews as a young Christian. I thought the opening sentence was the coolest thing ever I had ever read. I memorised it and began to say it every day.

*"Faith is the substance of things hoped for,
the evidence of things not seen". Hebrews 11 :1*

I did not realise it but every time I repeated it, I was actually fulfilling Romans 10:17.

Faith comes by hearing and hearing by the word.

One day it grabbed me. Faith in the word of God, turns hope in the word of God, into reality in the world of man. It is faith in the Word of God. Not natural human faith which is really more like 'will power'. Faith IS the substance NOW therefore faith is literally the word of God personified. Faith is Jesus. He is the very essence and spirit of faith. Glory to God!

How does David relate to Waw? On this occasion it is difficult to say. However, we do have some clues. There are two key words; Mercy and Salvation. This stanza begins with a plea for mercy. This may be because mercy was the hook that God used in David's life. Perhaps it is one of the things that he hangs his faith upon. Conversely, our hook would be grace through Jesus Christ.

For the law was given through Moses, but grace and truth came through Jesus Christ. John 1 : 17

Grace is unmerited favour. A bestowal that we did not qualify for. Mercy on the other hand, is not a gift but an act. Mercy is shielding its recipient from receiving an injustice or punishment. This is why David cries out for it in faith since he could not yet be made perfect through the blood of Christ. He is under the law of Moses. He sees the ultimate hook as salvation and therefore makes his plea for this also. Remember, this was David's idea of salvation. Do bear in mind that Christ has not yet been revealed. In David's day, Calvary was just a dusty hill called Golgotha in Jerusalem waiting for its destiny to be fulfilled. Unlike the free gift of salvation which we have been given, David must instead cry out continually for mercy from God. Clearly, his "hooks" will be different to ours but we can relate through the Holy Spirit.

In conclusion, Waw, the hook, is part of the nature of God. Waw is the strength that binds us to Him and by which all things are held together. From Waw, mentioned in God's name, ultimately we learn that the Word (Jesus Christ) is the hook or revelation that we can safely hang our faith upon. He is eternal yet He is practical. He is huge enough to hold all things together by His word. Yet He is involved in our everyday lives. He keeps the universe in the palm of His hand like a toy, yet He underpins our lives and gives us structure. He is the substance of faith which makes our hopes become reality. Yet He is our friend and help in time of trouble. He is adhesive and magnetic ever drawing more and more people to His love using the hook of His power to change the very fabric of our lives. Waw is seemingly insignificant in size but yet is a powerhouse of revelation which we can only begin to touch on in this study.

The Waw Prayer

Lord we thank you for your indestructible word which holds heaven and earth together. We thank you that all things are held together by your word and without your word, nothing exists. Thank you for the testimony of the Holy Spirit who brings to our remembrance every word that we can safely hang our faith on. And thank you for your son, the Word which became flesh and dwells in us. Amen

The Seventh Letter

Jesus the Aleph Tav

ZAYIN

Jesus the Aleph Tav

CHAPTER 7

ZAYIN
The Sword of the Lord

*Remember the word to Your servant, upon which You have
caused me to hope.
This is my comfort in my affliction, for Your word
has given me life.
The proud have me in great derision, yet I do not turn aside
from Your law.
I remembered Your judgments of old, O Lord,
And have comforted myself.
Indignation has taken hold of me
Because of the wicked, who forsake Your law.
Your statutes have been my songs
In the house of my pilgrimage. I remember Your name in the
night, O Lord, And I keep Your law.
This has become mine, Because I kept Your precepts.
Psalms 119 : 49-56*

For the word of God is living and powerful, and sharper than any two-edged sword, piercing even to the division of soul and spirit, and of joints and marrow, and is a discerner of the thoughts and intents of the heart. Hebrews 4:12

I thought we would just go ahead and start this letter with a scripture which defines it perfectly. We could equally go to the sixth chapter of Ephesians where the Apostle Paul is describing the armour of God. In verse 17b He eloquently describes the word of God, as the sword of the Spirit. We can clearly see from these two scriptures that the Apostle Paul had a very clear revelation about this particular letter. Sometimes it is easy to forget the fact that the majority of the early apostles came from a Jewish extraction. The knowledge which we are searching for in our study of the Hebrew letters would have been commonplace to many in the time of Christ. Zayin was hieroglyphically drawn as a sword. We have therefore interpreted it as the sword of the Lord.

Our opening scripture from Hebrews highlights a character of the word of God often missed. Let us break it down to its Christ like elements. Firstly it is described as double edged or two edged. This is giving us a sense of the bi-lateral nature of the word. I believe this is pointing to the fact that the word of God operates in the earth with exactly the same power and authority as it does in Heaven. Whether the angle of swing is up or down, it will cut all matter perfectly! Glory to God.

Paul describes the word of God's ability to pierce and divide both soul and spirit and joints and marrow. I laboured with this thought for many days before receiving what I am about to say. I believe the key to understanding the statement, will depend primarily on where you will place your division. You may for example, see two separate divisions. The first being the word of God dividing soul and spirit and then secondly you may see it dividing joints and marrow. This isn't about right or wrong but I am not sure that this is the way the apostle wanted us to read his words. I think it is more likely that he was expressing the word of God's ability to divide these two groups of related but separate matter. (Metaphysical and Physical or Spiritual and Natural). In simple terms, the first group would be soul and spirit and the second would be joints and marrow. If you think about it carefully, what he appears to be saying to us, is the word of God has the ability to separate us from our natural selves , allowing us to see ourselves the way that God created us, in the spirit. Glory be to God.

With this revelation we find the first and most important picture of Christ that Zayin gives us. The moment He comes into our lives as our saviour, Christ begins to show us who we really are or rather who we were meant to be in the spirit!

Paul then goes on to say that the word of God is a discerner of the thoughts and intentions of the heart. What a concept! These are living words that you can read which have a double effect. Whilst you are reading the word, the word is reading you! This means we always get exactly what we need or do not need at the time of engagement with the word.

Bearing the aforementioned in mind, in the sixth chapter of Ephesians, the apostle Paul explains to us in greater detail exactly why we need a sword that is able to operate in the spirit realm.

"For we do not wrestle against flesh and blood, but against principalities, against powers, against the rulers of the darkness of this age, against spiritual hosts of wickedness in the heavenly places". Ephesians 6:12.

If there is one thing our enemy is good at, it must be camouflage. Surreptitiously hiding his work behind the actions of another human being, he effectively goads us against one another. This is possibly one of his greatest strategies against man and particularly the born again Christian. If he can bring discord and disunity into our lives, he knows he will disturb the flow of blessing and anointing apportioned to us. We must not let him win. We must learn to use our sword of the Spirit to strike down every deadly blow of the enemy.

More importantly we need to learn how to use our sword, not just defensively but on the attack. En garde! Lunge! How do we do that? By using the word of God in a pre-emptive way, confessing its power and benefits over ours and our families lives every single day, without fail. God created the Heavens and the Earth, our dwelling place with His word. Equally, I believe we create our dwelling-place and the conditions that we will live under with our words. The book of Isaiah says "And He has made My mouth like a sharp sword;" Isaiah 49:2. How does the tongue of a man become like the sword of the Lord? When that man is speaking the word of God. I submit to you, in conclusion, that any person with a revelation of the power of God's word as a sword is an extreme danger to the work of the enemy. Like Christ, He empowers us with dynamic ability to make the devil's efforts against us futile.

What about the Davidic perspective on Zayin? He opens this stanza with the words.

"Remember the word to Your servant, upon which You have caused me to hope. This is my comfort in my affliction, for Your word has given me life" .

As I was writing these words the Lord whispered a single word in my ear. "Promise". God's promises were David's greatest treasure of hope. But why is he asking God to remember His word? In the book of Isaiah, the Lord says,

"Put Me in remembrance; Let us contend together; State your case, that you may be acquitted." Isaiah 43:26

In other words: remind Me of what I have said. Not because I have forgotten, but because I want you to remember what I have promised you so together we can make our stand on it. God wants us then to use our Zayin by faith to contend in unity with His word (Him) so that we may be acquitted. *(An acquittal is a judgement or verdict that a person is not guilty of the crime for which they have been charged).*

Beloved friends, I believe every negative circumstance which we face as believers, comes as a result of satan's continual charges against God's children. Further, for every blessing, there is a reverse curse. For every promise there is a reverse lie. The battle we face, sometimes daily, is simply getting this into perspective. We need the sword of the spirit to divide us from ourselves. We need it to give us a heavenly perspective of the battles we face. Only then can we be positioned to defeat the mortal enemy of our souls by fighting the battles we should be fighting whilst simultaneously side-stepping the carnal distractions. I know this is hard but we need to heed these words very carefully as they will save us the useless, endless pain, suffering and time wasting resulting from fighting carnal battles with other people.   Whether it is: Jobs, employers, family members, church leaders friends or enemies. Always remember the following:

"For the weapons of our warfare are not carnal but mighty in God for pulling down strongholds, casting down arguments and every high thing that exalts itself against the knowledge of God, bringing every thought into captivity to the obedience of Christ", 2cor 10:4

Amen.

The Zayin Prayer

Heavenly Father, thank you for your word. According to Ephesians 6:17, we are to arm ourselves with the sword of the Spirit, which is the word of God. Help us to exercise our faith in your word to fight our battles and to see ourselves as you see us. Help us to discern between battles that are worth fighting and the ones we should walk away from.

Amen

The Eighth Letter

Jesus the Aleph Tav

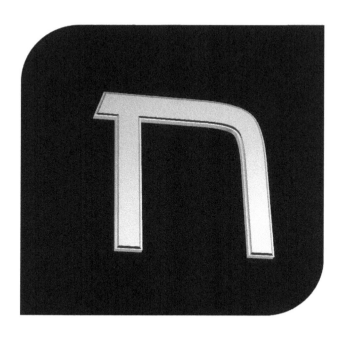

HETH

Jesus the Aleph Tav

CHAPTER 8

HETH
The Hedge or Fence

You are my portion, O Lord; I have said that I would keep Your
words. I entreated Your favor with my whole heart;
Be merciful to me according to Your word.
I thought about my ways, And turned my feet to
Your testimonies. I made haste, and did not delay
To keep Your commandments.
The cords of the wicked have bound me,
But I have not forgotten Your law.
At midnight I will rise to give thanks to You,
Because of Your righteous judgments.
I am a companion of all who fear You,
And of those who keep Your precepts.
The earth, O Lord, is full of Your mercy;
Teach me Your statutes.

Psalms 119 : 57- 64

The eighth Hebrew letter brings yet another wonderful revelation of God's goodness and kindness towards us. Heth was hieroglyphically drawn as a fence or hedge and so it firstly speaks to us of God's protection. The 125th Psalm carries a beautiful illustration of this.

'As the mountains surround Jerusalem so the Lord surrounds his people from this time forth and forever'   Psalms 125:2

We understand that from the day we accepted the Lord Jesus Christ as our saviour, He brought us His grace and favour. This is evident. However, in addition to this, He also brought us His protection. Let us note some key words of this stanza.

'I entreated your favour with my whole heart, be merciful to me according to your word.' Psalm 119 : 58

The Hebrew word for 'mercy" is Hannan. It begins with the letter Heth. It carries the sense of surrounding and covering. Note the way in which King David used this prayer. Particularly, the following phrase. "I thought about my ways, And turned my feet to your testimonies."

He continues to say that the cords of the wicked have bound

me. What is he saying exactly? I believe what we see here is a picture of a man who has sinned and come to his senses. Hence the words, I thought about my ways. This man then cries out to God for mercy, which in this sense means to encamp or surround.

David is asking God to surround and protect him from the wicked who are attacking him as a result of his sin. As we already have seen in the 6th letter Waw, mercy is a cry for protection, to be shielded from the ramifications of our own sins or the wrath of another.

In the most holy place, contained in the tabernacle of Moses, there was the Ark of the covenant. It had a beautiful lid which was made of acacia wood overlaid with pure gold. There were two Cherubim angels with their wings outstretched above it and their faces looking down to the place where the sacrificial blood would be poured. The lid was called the mercy seat. It was the place where the high priests confessed the sins of Israel and where they in turn received mercy and forgiveness from God. God responded in kind and fenced them from harm. David's request in verse 58 is merely a snapshot of the entire of Psalm 59 which is completely devoted to the concept of God's defence through his mercy.

Let us now examine one of David's closing remarks in verse 62.

"At midnight I will rise to give thanks to you".

As I was reading this, I wondered whether Heth is leading us to another great revealing. I refer to the relationship between prayer and the protection of God. In my early days of Christianity, I attended a Pentecostal church in East London, England. One of the songs we sang regularly was;

Jesus be a fence all around me every day. Lord I want you to protect me as I travel along the way. Lord I know you can, Lord I know you will, fight my battles if I just keep still. Be a fence all around me every day..

I wonder whether the writers of that chorus actually understood what they were writing? Perhaps they were aware of the significance of the Aleph Tav in Psalm 119, in particular the Heth connection. I can remember attending many prayer gatherings where we often held hands around the sanctuary as we sang this refrain. I can still see the faces of the mothers and elderly sisters in the church as they smiled shaking each others hands vigorously as if they were literally receiving the protection from the Lord as they sang. Then one day I heard one of my favourite preachers delivering a sermon from the book of Ecclesiastes.

*'He that digs a pit shall fall into it and who ever breaks a
hedge a serpent shall bite him' Ecclesiastes 10:8*

I suddenly remembered those sisters holding hands in a circle. It was a hedge of protection. They would not let go of one another. No one would break the hedge! Dear ones, I believe we break the hedge when we lose faith in the fact that Jesus is our protector. As long as you hold onto that revelation, and believe that the hedge is there to protect, you are safe. Similarly, the hedge being referred to by David, may be the hedge of a particular type of prayer. He says he will rise at midnight, inferring that he has already retired to sleep. Could David be hinting to us that making a sacrifice of his personal sleep time to give thanks to God brought him a special layer of protection from the Father?

My Auntie, Esther Stead, was one of those sisters praying earnestly for the salvation of her family members, including me! She never broke the fence, and one day, many years later I would experience the power of her prayer in my own life.

When I was in my 20's I worked for a large newspaper group in London called the Observer. I seemed to have the gift of the gab and consequently became quite successful as a salesperson.

One day, my line manager wanted to celebrate the fact that I had become his top salesperson and invited me to go away for the weekend to a pop festival. I had arranged to meet him on the next Friday evening at 9 pm at King's Cross station, where I would be picked up in a van with some other friends of his. I went home on the Friday with every intention of going on the trip. I was feeling a little tired after work and the journey home so I sat down to gather my thoughts first. I closed my eyes for what seemed to be a matter of two or three minutes and then opened them again. To my surprise I saw my answering machine blinking with 11 missed messages. I thought to myself, that is impossible. How could I have missed 11 messages? For I knew that I had only shut my eyes for a matter of moments. Somehow time seem to have jumped five hours ahead and it was now far too late for me to go on the trip. I listened to the messages which confirmed that my rather upset manager left without me. This was back in August of 1986, some years before the advent of mobile telephony. I felt so foolish to have missed out on what was described to me as an opportunity of a lifetime. I was equally upset with myself for missing out on an opportunity to bond with my manager for the weekend. In that world at the time, it was felt that this kind of thing was very important if you were looking for a promotion of any kind. After an uneventful weekend and three good nights sleep I woke up early on Monday morning. I opened my eyes with a strange eerie feeling. My portable television automatically came on at 7 am as normal with the morning news. Within moments, I was wide awake and witnessing the aftermath of a horrific motorway crash. There were live pictures of an overturned coach which had come to rest on top of a mangled blue van. As I laid in bed watching my portable TV, I suddenly received a chilling thought. One that I could not shake off. "You would have been in the van". When I got to work that morning, I told everyone about my premonition. Then I realised my manager had not arrived at work. At mid-day, our Director came to the office to make the very sad announcement. I already knew what he was going to say, and so did half of the department. The driver and all of the passengers in the blue van had perished. Beloved friends, there was due to be one more passenger in that vehicle. I did not make it. This was 10 years before I would come into a relationship with Jesus, yet, He put me into a supernatural sleep and consequently I missed the van. God put a hedge around me and fenced me in from destruction. It still took me 10 years before I would come into a relationship with Christ, because I had no idea what God had done for me. I write these words in the hope that someone someday, may read them and be prompted to examine his or her own life. How many times do you suppose that God has saved your life from destruction?

Heth is the fence of protection that saved me that day by putting me to sleep. Now I know the Lord, I know Jesus is my protector and furthermore according to Psalms 103 verse 4, He is ever redeeming my life from destruction every day.

Heth represents the hedge or fence - As a hedge may surround a building or home, Heth is constantly reminding us of the truth that we are protected from the hand of the enemy through the shedding of the blood of Jesus Christ. It also reminds us of the presence of mighty Angels of God sent to protect the children of the Lord.

Has the Lord protected you? Write your testimony here:

The Heth Prayer

Heavenly Father, thank you that we can rely on you for protection. Not only for ourselves but also for our family and friends. We are at peace knowing that you watch over us as we go out and return and that your hedge of protection constantly surrounds us in Christ.

Amen

The Ninth Letter

TETH

Jesus the Aleph Tav

CHAPTER 9

TETH
The Serpent

You have dealt well with Your servant, O Lord,
according to Your word.
Teach me good judgment and knowledge,
for I believe Your commandments.
Before I was afflicted I went astray, but now I keep Your word.
You are good, and do good; Teach me Your statutes.
The proud have forged a lie against me, but I will keep Your
precepts with my whole heart.
Their heart is as fat as grease, but I delight in Your law.
It is good for me that I have been afflicted,
that I may learn Your statutes.
The law of Your mouth is better to me than thousands of coins
of gold and silver.

Psalms 119 : 65 - 72

In my introduction, I have stated that every stanza of Psalms 119 is an allegory of the word of God and therefore of Christ. Consequently many of you will be most surprised by the hieroglyphic root of this letter which as you can see is the serpent.

Our Hebraic studies revealed an important truth about this letter which must be noted in order to understand the connection to the serpent. Teth also alludes to mud or dirt. The very thing, according to the Bible, from which God created man. Teth therefore also represents the flesh or fleshiness (natural man as compared to the spiritual). Now with that understanding in place, let us bury the obvious connection to satan and try to understand what is being revealed here. Teth is actually a picture of the way God helps us to overcome the flesh through His word.

We must journey to the Old Testament, specifically the book of Numbers 21, in order to under-gird this truth. In this chapter we find Moses and the children of Israel during their exodus from Egypt. The chapter highlights the fact that after some time in the wilderness the people began to become discouraged. They began to murmur and backbite against Moses saying things like; "Have you brought us up out of Egypt to die in the wilderness?" They complained because they had no bread or water. God had sent them manna to eat but they complained saying we loath this light bread.

'And the Lord sent fiery serpents among the people, and they bit the people; and much people of Israel died. Therefore the people came to Moses, and said, We have sinned, for we have spoken against the Lord, and against thee; pray unto the Lord, that He take away the serpents from us. And Moses prayed for the people. And the Lord said unto Moses, Make thee a fiery serpent, and set it upon a pole: and it shall come to pass, that every one that is bitten, when he looks upon it, shall live'.
Numbers 21: 6 - 8

As we continue in this account, we read that Moses followed God's instructions to the letter. He made the serpent of brass. He placed it on a pole and it came to pass that if a serpent had bitten anyone, when he beheld the serpent of brass he lived. Given what we have learned thus far in our study, I do not think it is unreasonable to suppose that it was actually the letter Teth (or at least the symbol of it), that Moses modelled and raised in the wilderness. Whilst I cannot prove this absolutely, I do have another witness who shares the same opinion. Who is this witness? He is none other than the Lord Jesus Christ Himself. This is the direct reference to the account in the book of John.

'And as Moses lifted up the serpent in the wilderness, even so must the Son of man be lifted up: That whosoever believes in him should not perish, but have eternal life'. John 3 : 14 -15

There is an important key to seeing and understanding the deeply revealed truths from the Aleph Tav. I do not mind repeating this as many times as it takes. Jesus Christ was at all times fully cognisant of the fact that He is the word of God made flesh. Every reference that He makes about Himself reflects this. He does not just mindlessly pluck His sayings out of the air. He makes deep conclusive references to Himself in the first person for the purpose of allowing those with eyes to see and ears to hear, to recognise who He really is.

Let us look at the account so far. The people sinned. There was judgement from God. People started suffering and dying. The people appealed to Moses begging God to forgive them. Moses interceded for the people. God told Moses to make and lift the serpent up. Moses told the people to gaze at the serpent in faith. The people were healed.

Now let us look at the case of Christ today. There is only one way to be born again and that is to acknowledge Christ's sacrifice on the cross of Calvary. This is the lifting up that Jesus was referring to. The people had to look at the serpent (God's own solution for their sin) by faith. Today we must look to Christ by faith, in order to be saved.

The Jews murmured and complained against Moses who was God's chosen one, sent to help them. In the same way today, the world murmurs and complains against Jesus and indeed against His messengers. Daily, in all forms of media, the message of Christ is spurned. Hatred for the founding principles of God have reached the point where schools, governments and indeed entire nations are seeking to alienate the Gospel. They are choosing rather to follow secular humanist thinking, allowing for and favouring the desires of their own hearts. Remember in Aleph, He became our sacrifice. When Christ was nailed to the cross, He took the sin of mankind onto His own flesh. He did it so that we would not have to suffer the eternal punishment of sin. From that cross the Bible informs us that He cried the words "My God, My God why have you forsaken me?" In this, He depicts for us both the holiness and the love of God. God could not look at His beloved son whilst He was carrying our state of sin. However, we must look at Him. If we do not, we cannot be saved and must consequently suffer eternal damnation.

For He made Him who knew no sin to be sin for us, that we might become the righteousness of God in Him.
2 Corinthians 5:21

In comparing Himself to the serpent, Jesus is saying "If you can understand the purpose for My Father sending the serpent, you will understand His purpose in sending me".

Look at the similarities in both accounts. God sent the serpent as judgement. God sent His son for judgement. This is evidenced in John 9:39. The Jews had to repent, we have to repent. They had to look by faith, we must do so also. They received forgiveness, mercy and restoration to a good relationship with God and Moses. We likewise receive forgiveness, grace, mercy, restoration and a new relationship with God through Jesus!

Returning our attention to the stanza. I stated earlier, Teth the serpent, is actually a picture of the way God helps us to overcome the flesh through His word. Look at David's opening words.

"You have dealt well with your servant. "

I smile as I write the interpretation of these words. To my mind, David is saying "God, you know me so well. You understand that I was born in flesh and iniquity and that I cannot deal with myself. I cannot overcome my own failings. I cannot break my own will. I needed you to help me and now you have done it, I am satisfied and grateful". Glory to God! When you understand Teth, you can clearly hear David's heart. This is why he continues to say

Before I was afflicted I went astray, but now I keep Your word.

It is good for me that I have been afflicted, That I may learn Your statutes. Verses 67 & 71

I love to reverse engineer David's words because I believe this brings us greater clarity. Again, this is my interpretation.

I knew you but I was living a life astray and away from you my God. As a result of that, I became afflicted. I knew Your word was judging me. So I repented and came back to you and you forgave me. Thank you, for the afflictions that you allowed me to undergo, for they did not destroy me but were sufficient to cause me to re-assess my life and make a decision to follow after your heart and not my own. So effective was the nature of your handling of me that I will never stray again but rather I will follow after your word. Hallelujah.

In conclusion. You may feel that I have erred by alluding in this chapter to the possibility that God sends or allows the work of the enemy symbolised by the serpent to judge or punish us. I must tell you that I believe this is sometimes the case. However, He isn't judging us but solely our flesh. A good comparison would be a wild horse. Horses were essential to man before the development of other trans-portation vehicles, like cars and lorries. However, before the horse could be useful, it had to be broken.

This would have been very unpleasant for the horse, in fact I am sure after a time of strong resistance the beast would have realised that resistance was futile. In some ways ironically, it is in the area of the flesh that we must share the fate of the beast of burden. The flesh must be broken. The difference is that we are broken by the gentle hands of a master who has better uses for us than to merely gallop aimlessly through life. It is most important to note that God the Father does not destroy us but rather He delivers us from all the afflictions which were brought about by the failings of our flesh.

Many are the afflictions of the righteous, But the Lord delivers him out of them all. Psalm 34:19

I hope that you have enjoyed reading this chapter as much as I have enjoyed writing it. Teth carries such a huge revelation that it really deserves a book of its own! However, we must move onto the next letter and allow the Holy Spirit to further expand for you the thoughts that I have seeded in this passage. God bless you as you continue to read and study with me.

Finally, Teth reminds us of our route to salvation. We were born in iniquity with certain judgement awaiting until we receive the ultimate sacrifice at Calvary through which, we are all made free. It reminds us that Christ took the sin of the whole world upon Himself on the cross of Calvary.

The Teth Prayer

Lord Jesus we thank you for your victory over sin, over evil and over the devil. We declare through this prayer that we live in a place of triumph over all of his activities in our lives. We know that he has been defeated and no matter how things may appear, his presence is now illegal in our lives. Through Christ, we claim your victory over satan and his minions in your name.

Amen

The Tenth Letter

YOD

Jesus the Aleph Tav

CHAPTER 10

YOD
The open Hand of God

Your hands have made me and fashioned me; Give me understanding, that I may learn Your commandments. Those who fear You will be glad when they see me, Because I have hoped in Your word. I know, O Lord, that Your judgments are right, And that in faithfulness You have afflicted me. Let, I pray, Your merciful kindness be for my comfort, According to Your word to Your servant. Let Your tender mercies come to me, that I may live; For Your law is my delight. Let the proud be ashamed, For they treated me wrongfully with falsehood; But I will meditate on Your precepts. Let those who fear You turn to me, Those who know Your testimonies. Let my heart be blameless regarding Your statutes, That I may not be ashamed.

Psalms 119 : 73 - 80

Jesus the Aleph Tav

Welcome to our study of the tenth letter of the Hebrew alphabet. The letter YOD is a beautiful one indeed. One of the smallest letters, it could even be compared to an apostrophe or comma. Yod is the first constituent part of the name Yahweh / Jehovah. We will discuss this in more detail later on. Yod is symbolic of the hand or pointing finger. I add this because it is also the name of the stick used in Jewish synagogues to point to the scriptures as they are being read.

I believe Yod is an extremely important letter because there are so many spiritual and natural dimensions   associated with it. Every human being has 10 fingers. The Ten command-ments were written on stone tablets by the finger of God! The letter Yod, meaning 'hand', is the 10th letter!

There is a profoundly significant museum in western Jerusalem which honours the victims of the Holocaust. It is called Yad Vashem, meaning memorial place. Yad has exactly the same root and meaning as YOD. I interpret this as "The hand of God is on this place so you can remember. " If you ever have the opportunity to visit that place, I am sure you will sense His presence as I, and I am sure millions of others have.

David begins this stanza with the words "Your hands have made me and fashioned me". The implication here is closeness. Picture the hands of God working the clay and forming it into man. Picture Him then breathing life into the shape as He holds man in the palm of His hand. The hand is our instrument of touch. Our most intimate relationships are confirmed by touch.

Man, who is unlike a tree, a bird or a fish, (all of which simply exist by the word of His command), has been shaped by personal manifestation of the hands of God.

Yod teaches us that Jesus Christ was always cognisant of this fact. He is the word in manifestation. This is evidenced in the book of John chapter 8. Here we see Christ in the temple teaching the people on the Mount of Olives. The Scribes and Pharisees brought a woman to Him who they had caught in the very act of adultery. They said "Moses commanded in the law that she should be stoned but what do you say?" This was an attempt to discredit Jesus by getting Him to judge against the law. The Bible says that Christ simply stooped down and wrote on the ground with His finger as though He did not hear them. The crowd continued to press Him for an answer. For a while, He remained silent only writing with His finger and then the Bible declares that;

He raised Himself up and said to them, "He who is without sin among you, let him throw a stone at her first." And again He stooped down and wrote on the ground. Then those who heard it, being convicted by their conscience, went out one by one, beginning with the oldest even to the last. And Jesus was left alone, and the woman standing in the midst. John 8 : 7-9

Many people have presented theories about what Christ was writing on the ground. Many are extremely valid. For me, the most enthralling of these is from a book by Joe Amaral called Understanding Jesus. In his book, Joe remarks that Jesus was using "Remez", the rabbinic hinting method. According to the author, by writing on the ground, Jesus was alluding to Jeremiah.

O Lord, the hope of Israel,
All who forsake You shall be ashamed.
"Those who depart from Me
Shall be written in the earth,
Because they have forsaken the Lord,
The fountain of living waters." Jeremiah 17:13

Note the words "WRITTEN IN THE EARTH." Now back up to John 7:37 which chronicles the events which precede the incident with the woman caught in the act.

On the last day, that great day of the feast, Jesus stood and cried out, saying, "If anyone thirsts, let him come to Me and drink. He who believes in Me, as the Scripture has said, out of his heart will flow rivers of living water." John 7: 37-38

If you read on to verse 44, you can see that Jesus was rejected in exactly the same way Jeremiah had prophesied. A careful study of the Jewish feasts is necessary to understand the complete connection. For now we will stay focussed on the letter Yod. Where I slightly differ with Mr Amaral, is that I do not believe Christ is just doodling. Notwithstanding the aforementioned, I believe He is prophetically declaring the fact that He is the living word. The Yod of our lives. After all, Christ made a point of writing more than once so to me both theories stand.

Consider now, the wisdom and authority that Christ used in this passage. I love the words "He raised himself up." I believe His words sent chills to the very core of all who heard them. Such was the authority and power transmitted by them that they were all immediately ashamed. His words and actions seemed somehow to convey that these were the very hands which made them all. Another beautiful Remez hint is found in this very stanza. David writes in verse 78, "Let the proud be ashamed". They certainly were. For more information about pardez and the principles associated with 'remez', go to the back of this book where you will find a short chapter about the principle in the glossary.

The hand of God also speaks of His mighty presence. This was evident in the earliest days of the church where incredible miracles were being performed everywhere by the disciples of Jesus. The first mention of such power was in a place called Antioch. It is accounted in Hebrews 11:21 that the hand of the Lord was with them. Consequently, this was the first place where believers inherited the title Christian. Praise the Lord, Christianity began with the presence of the hand of God.

Those of you who see significance in numbers will also note that Psalm 89:21 highlights yet another usage of the letter Yod. Quoted in first person, God says;

"I have found my servant David; With my holy oil I have anointed him. With whom my hand shall be established, also my arm shall strengthen him". Psalm 89:20-21.

This passage teaches us that the hand of God is present with those who have received the Holy Spirit. We know this because the anointing is literally the presence of God through the Holy Spirit. For more information about this subject you could also get my forthcoming book called Anointer, Anointing,

Anointed. God, the Holy Spirit and you.

I am going to use three P's to help us understand the wonderful benefits associated with the hand of God. The first 'P', stands for Power. His power is present through his hand. We just saw this in the book of Acts. The second 'P', is for Provision. His provision will never be far away through His hand. Now the final 'P' is for Path. This comes from the revelation of the pointing stick. He shows us a clear path to our destiny in Him as long as we follow His word.

Yahweh / Jehovah

Now we have studied the three elements which make up the hidden name of God. These are Yod, He, Waw, He. This was then shortened by the Jews to YHWH. Yahweh was westernised as Jehovah. Now you understand the ancient Hebrew meanings, you might want to meditate on what we have studied thus far. As you do, I believe you will begin to see the Father God in a whole new light of understanding.

In Conclusion, Yod reminds us that we need not fight our own battles because His presence is ever with us to aid us. It also teaches us that God will guide us to the word through the Holy Spirit who is the very living Yod of our lives.

The Yod Prayer

*Lord what a delight it is to know that through Jesus Christ
your hand is always with us. As we go through so many
different circumstances, we know that we are not alone.
Your strength and power is always present in our lives
making the impossible possible and the unreachable
reachable through faith in your word. Lord, As your hand
was with the early church at Antioch and with your
Anointed, ever let it also be with us.*

Amen

The Eleventh Letter

KAPH

Jesus the Aleph Tav

CHAPTER 11

KAPH
The Wing or Palm of God

My soul faints for Your salvation, But I hope in Your word.
My eyes fail from searching Your word,
Saying, "When will You comfort me?"
For I have become like a wineskin in smoke,
Yet I do not forget Your statutes.
How many are the days of Your servant?
When will You execute judgment on those who persecute me?
The proud have dug pits for me, Which is not according to Your
law. All Your commandments are faithful;
They persecute me wrongfully; Help me!
They almost made an end of me on earth,
But I did not forsake Your precepts.
Revive me according to Your lovingkindness,
So that I may keep the testimony of Your mouth.
Psalms 119 : 81 - 88

The Hebrew letter Kaph has a double meaning. Originally and hieroglyphically depicted as a wing, it equally carries the sense of a cupped hand. For those in Christ, the Messiah, Kaph delivers for us a double portion of blessing as we study it. Under either definition, the interpretation of it remains consistent. Kaph speaks of covering. (The shape can be formed by placing your hand upon your own head.)

"Therefore humble yourselves under the mighty hand of God, that He may exalt you in due time, casting all your care upon Him, for He cares for you". 1Peter 5:6

THE CUPPED HAND

Kaph carries a very different sense to Yod (alluding to power), which we covered in our last chapter. Koph literally speaks of God's divine hand being upon His children for the purpose of authority, responsibility and protection. A good way to understand the letter in this sense, is to think about holiday insurance. If you were to go away on a family vacation without insurance, there may be a slight worry in the back of your mind. "What if I lose my luggage, or something gets stolen". In this case, it would be a complete loss. However, if you were to take out holiday insurance, you would be travelling with a sense of peace. This is because you would know that whatever happens, the insurance company will underwrite your losses. This is basically what the covering of God brings to us. We have the assurance of His hand of protection over us in every circumstance we face.

A wonderful Jewish illustration of this covering is to be gained from a study of the Bar Mitzvah tradition. This is where a 13-year-old Jewish boy will undergo an ancient coming of age ritual. During the ceremony, he will receive his first kippa. This is a small Jewish cap worn at the top of the skull, symbolising the fact that the young man has come of age. The Bar Mitzvah also symbolises the fact that from the day the boy was born until the age of 13, he was actually under the covering (or the insurance policy) of his parents. According to Jewish law, when he reaches the age of 13, they may no longer remain his covering. He must take responsibility for himself before God. From this day forth, he is therefore considered mature enough to read the Torah for himself and create his own relationship with God.

As Christians, we come of age the day we give our lives to Jesus. From that moment on we, through the Holy Spirit, begin to develop our relationship directly with God. It is as if we are wearing a kippa standing under the Kaph of God.

THE WING

When presented as the wing, Kaph gives us a slightly different perspective. We can get this quite clearly by looking at the two following scriptures which at first glance, do not appear to be related. We look firstly to the book of Exodus, where we find again, the instructions given to Moses concerning the construction of the Mercy Seat, which we have previously looked at with the letter Heth. Moses was commanded to build a box out of acacia wood. He was then to overlay it with pure gold. His next task, was to construct two angels or cherubim to be placed at the head and foot of the box. They were to have large outstretched wings leaning forward toward each other so that they met in the middle. Most importantly, their faces were to look downwards at the Mercy Seat. I was once in a prayer meeting where in the midst I was shown a vision of what looked like a crude figure 8 made of gold. The shape was covering a golden plate. I viewed this from above. As I prayed it through I realised I was looking at the wings of the two Cherubim above the Ark of the Covenant. It was the wings which formed the figure 8.

Now we need to journey beyond Calvary where we find Mary Magdalene, weeping at the place where Christ had been entombed. Here she finds not the body of Christ but rather two angels.

'But Mary stood outside by the tomb weeping, and as she wept she stooped down and looked into the tomb. And she saw two angels in white sitting, one at the head and the other at the feet, where the body of Jesus had lain.' John 20 : 11-12

Pay close attention to the position of the angels. Do you see it? One at the head, the other at the feet. The Cherubim Angels covered the Mercy Seat. That was the place where the sacrificial blood was sprinkled to save the children of Israel. The angels also covered the body of Christ in the tomb. What were they doing? They were watching over the precious blood of Jesus. Even after He was raised, they watched over His shed blood. Some of which must have remained in the tomb. We know this because the Bible tells us that they were watching over the place where Christ had been laid. In a sense, His stone bed inside the tomb had become the new Mercy Seat. Not just for the children of Israel but for all of mankind. Now this brings me to the third covering. I believe angels cover and protect those who have received the great sacrifice of the blood of Jesus Christ. Our lives are marked with his blood.

'Are they not all ministering spirits sent forth to minister for those who will inherit salvation?' Hebrews 1:14

'The angel of the Lord encamps all around those who fear Him, And delivers them.' Psalms 34.7

*"But to you who fear My name, the Sun of Righteousness shall
arise with healing in His wings" ; Malachi 4:2
(Example of healing Kaph)*

Perhaps the woman with the issue of blood knew this scripture for she broke Judaic law in order to push through the
crowd and touch the hem (Hebrew Kanaph, or wing) of Christ's
garment to receive her total healing instantly. When she did
this, Christ said "I felt virtue leaving me". It was that woman's
faith making a withdrawal on His power ! Let us consider one
more scripture:

*Bless the Lord, you His angels,Who excel in strength, who do His
word, Heeding the voice of His word. Bless the Lord, all you His
hosts,You ministers of His, who do His pleasure.
Psalm 103 : 20-21*

David begins this Chapter with the words "My soul faints
for your salvation." He also ends the Stanza with a plea for
physical revival. This is clear from the Hebrew root study.
Koph, the wing, brings us a special sense of God's presence manifesting His will through angels. This is actually
the meaning of one of the Hebrew names for God, Elohim.
Meaning God's plural presence through angels. David would
have understood this and so he makes his plea accordingly.

I believe Kaph highlights the Lord's desire and ability to touch and help His children in this physical world, through the presence of His mighty angels. I believe after you read the following account, you may believe it also.

I enjoyed many years of being a co-presenter of the Bible Study programme on Revelation TV. Every Monday, I drove from our home in Northamptonshire to New Malden to record the programmes. On one particular Monday, I was driving on a single carriageway road. (Meaning there is no protective bollard between oncoming and outgoing traffic). I was approaching a town called Olney. (Ironically, the town from which the song 'Amazing Grace' hailed). It was a very clear day, the sun was shining and I was, as usual, using my hands free headphones to make phone calls. I generally did this to stay awake on long journeys. Suddenly, out of that clear blue sky a huge bird swooped down in front of my car. This was about the biggest bird that I have ever seen. I am not an ornithologist but I would guess it was something like an Albatross or an Eagle. This bird started behaving very strangely in front of my car. I was driving at approximately 60-70 mph. The bird was flying approximately 30 feet in front of me. You can imagine my surprise as it began to mimic my car movements. When I turned even slightly to the left, it did the same. I turned to the right, it did also. I thought to myself "This is absolutely bizarre". This huge bird then did something that took me completely by surprise. To be honest it scared me a little. It suddenly thrust its wings outward using them like a huge pair of aircraft brakes. With this action it seemed to freeze in mid air. I was now heading straight for it.

In a split second, I had no choice but to slam on the brakes. The bird flew away whilst I was shocked and shaken. I ended my phone call and began to drive again when the absolutely unthinkable happened. The bird came back! Then after approximately 30 seconds of mimicking, it did exactly the same thing again. I slammed on my breaks a second time. Now I am thinking, "This is spiritual! But who is doing this to me? Is it the devil or is it God?" There is something supernatural happening. I started my car again and now drove slowly forward. I reached approximately 50 mph and once again my winged visitor emerged. This time immediately applying its air brakes, so that its wings slapped violently against my windscreen. As I brought my car to a halt, I was literally shaking. Just as I began to pull myself together, two cars appeared in my distant vision. They were getting closer and closer very quickly. I suddenly understood what was happening. The two cars were having a race. They were hurtling toward me on the single carriageway, which meant that one of them was driving in my lane. I knew there would be no way I could survive a head on collision. The driver of the red Lamborghini suddenly hit his brakes. Thank God, he must have realised that unless

someone had stopped, there would have been a terrible acci-
dent. This gave the blue BMW driver in my lane just enough
space to overtake him and thereby pass me. These guys were
playing a game of 'chicken', using my life as the bait! My car
which by now was completely stationary, shook violently with
the centrifugal force of both cars whizzing by. I sat quietly in
shock and began to praise God for saving me once again. I
watched the two cars vanishing into the distance in my rear
view mirror. Alive, unharmed and well able to share my story
today. Had it not been for the wing of God's protection, I would
have stood no chance of survival.

In conclusion, Kaph speaks of covering by the cupped hand of
God and also provides us with a sense of His incredible company
of protective angels, which are daily ministering His love and
protection to us. Kaph really carries another wonderful revelation of the presence of God in our lives through Jesus Christ.

The Kaph Prayer

Thank you Holy Spirit for teaching us the power of submission and humility. Lord, we know it is part of your plan for us to grow to perfection even through our difficult circumstances. We thank you that whilst we are in the season of learning and growing, we may be vulnerable. We are confident that during these times, you have provided Angelic protection for us.

Amen

The Twelfth Letter

Jesus the Aleph Tav

LAMED

CHAPTER 12

LAMED
The Goading Stick

Forever, O Lord, Your word is settled in heaven.
Your faithfulness endures to all generations;
You established the earth, and it abides.
They continue this day according to Your ordinances,
For all are Your servants.
Unless Your law had been my delight,
I would then have perished in my affliction. I will never forget
Your precepts, For by them You have given me life. I am Yours,
save me;
For I have sought Your precepts. The wicked wait for me to
destroy me, But I will consider Your testimonies.
I have seen the consummation of all perfection,
But Your commandment is exceedingly broad.
Psalms 119 : 89 - 96

I have been so blessed during my time of studying all of these wonderful Hebrew concepts in Psalm 119. Of all the letters which we studied, I seemed to relate to Lamed most of all.

Lamed was drawn in the shape of what was understood as a goading stick. When I first heard about this I did not understand what this meant. Visually, it looks like the top of a Shepherd's staff which was, in fact, used for the same purpose. Many of them had a sharp prod at the end which was used for sticking into the hide of a disobedient animal like a sheep or goat. You may immediately feel that this description is bordering on animal cruelty. Not so! These prods were designed to force direction without harming the cattle. They might have felt a bit sore when they were prodded but never put in mortal danger. Our dear friend Christine grew up in South Africa. As a child she saw a lot of sheep on the farms. Christine told us that they were the dumbest animals she had ever seen. Every now and then one would just go wandering off aimlessly and would have to be brought back to pasture. She could fully understand why a Shepherd would need to use some type of goading stick. Interesting isn't it? That believers are most often described in scripture as sheep in need of a Shepherd!

Perhaps you thought as I did, that the word goad was about forcing or irritating someone into a fight, which is largely the way I had heard it used. For example, someone might say "He goaded me into a fight". It may be necessary to lay that thought aside for now as it will seriously blur your understanding of this letter. Jewish theologians on the other hand, translate Lamed differently. They say it literally means "to teach". Whilst this can obviously be said of any of the 22 Hebrew letters, this definition will become much clearer as we study the rest of this stanza.

So how does the word of God teach us? I remember reading about a particular Shepherd who had a 3 prod system of goading. When the sheep gets out of line the first time, the Shepherd will give it a single prod. The sheep will feel the pain but not understand why. Sure enough, the sheep with curious tendencies will attempt to wander aimlessly off again. At this point, it receives a second prod. This time, it can relate the pain to the first prod. The Shepherd wants the sheep to understand that every time it wanders off it will feel the same pain. If the sheep gets the message it will not need a third prod however, if the message is ignored, the Shepherd has no choice but to deliver a third, much stronger prod. This one usually does the trick, and the sheep bleats its way back into line. Occasionally a Shepherd may find that a particularly obstinate sheep will kick back at the goading stick! In this case it will take a few more prods in order to convince him to stay on course. Does this sound at all familiar? Do not worry if it does. You are not alone. Take a look at this excerpt from the life of a man named

Saul who became the great Apostle Paul.

As he journeyed he came near Damascus, and suddenly a light shone around him from heaven. Then he fell to the ground, and heard a voice saying to him, "Saul, Saul, why are you persecuting Me?" And he said, "Who are You, Lord?" Then the Lord said, "I am Jesus, whom you are persecuting. It is hard for you to kick against the goads."
Acts 9 : 3-5

Note the words it is hard for you to kick against the goads or some versions say 'pricks'. Now that we understand the meaning of the goading Lamed, we can understand much more about Saul who became Paul. I do not know about you, but I had absolutely no idea what was meant by the term "kicking against the pricks or goads". Now we all do. We can now also understand that God had been working on Saul for some time previously to his encounter on the road to Damascus. Clearly, we now also understand that God had been goading him. And that Paul (like the obstinate sheep) on the other hand was resisting the goads or pricks. You may find that this understanding will allow you to see Saul in a new light. Now I see him not just as the persecutor and wrecker of the church, which he was. I now envisage one who loved God, and in turn, needed to be goaded into His perfect plan for his life.

'The words of the wise are like goads, and the words of scholars are like well-driven nails, given by one Shepherd'.
Ecclesiastes 12:11

We can now understand what the aforementioned scripture means. We may have to hear them a few times but each time we do they seem to nudge us in the right direction. Note again: The deliver of the word in this case is the Shepherd. The one who uses the goading stick.

David's take on Lamed

He opens with the words, "Forever oh Lord your word is settled in Heaven". This is to give us the sense that there is no point fighting against God's word. It is settled, finished, absolute and perfect. This says everything we need to hear. Then in verses 92 and 93. We get a real sense of his understanding of the goading and growing through the word of God.

Unless your law had been my delight, I would then have perished in my affliction. I will never forget your precepts.

I believe the Psalmist is saying that the law of God goaded him and goaded him. Eventually he heard and was delivered from his affliction. So is God the one behind the affliction? No! God isn't bringing the affliction but he is aware of it. His purpose through it is to teach His children how they may be delivered from it, forever.

Finally I want to draw our attention to one more pertinent fact. I know that I have said this before but please do remember as you study these letters, that Jesus was ALWAYS fully cognisant of who He is. I hope that now you will be also! He is the word of God who became flesh. In this scripture He is saying "I am the good Shepherd because I am Lamed". It was not just that He was speaking to Shepherds and wanted to identify with them. Although this may not be incorrect, it is incomplete! More than anything, the Lord was identifying Himself with these 22 Hebrew letters because He is the Aleph Tav.

In conclusion I say this. Lamed teaches us that Jesus Christ, through the Holy Spirit, is indeed our teacher. When we stray from His commandments, He lovingly guides us back to the right path by goading us. How does He do this? By His word. Despise not His chastening. He only corrects us because He loves us and wants God's best for our lives and for all eternity.

The Lamed Prayer

Lord Jesus, thank you for being the Good Shepherd of our lives. That you are not one who will leave us when the wolf attacks. When we go astray you guide us firmly and lovingly back onto the good path. May we be able to hear your voice of correction and heed your instructions through the presence of the Holy Spirit.

Amen

The Thirteenth Letter

MEM

CHAPTER 13

MEM
The Water of the Word

Oh, how I love Your law! It is my meditation all the day. You, through Your commandments, make me wiser than my enemies; For they are ever with me.
I have more understanding than all my teachers, For Your testimonies are my meditation.
I understand more than the ancients, Because I keep Your precepts.
I have restrained my feet from every evil way, That I may keep Your word.
I have not departed from Your judgments, For You Yourself have taught me. How sweet are Your words to my taste, Sweeter than honey to my mouth!
Through Your precepts I get understanding; Therefore I hate every false way.

Psalms 119 : 97 - 104

MEM speaks to us of water. When God made the world, the first thing we see recorded in scripture, is the Spirit of God hovering over the face of the waters. Water is profoundly important in creation, in the word of God and in our lives today. Like Christ Himself, every believer must be baptised as a great sign of our faith. This is our witness in Heaven, earth and beyond.

The word of God is absolutely filled with references to water. There are many direct comparisons of water to the word of God. Water cleanses, the word of God cleanses. Water is essential for the correct functionality of the body. The word of God is essential for the correct functionality of the body of Christ. The Earth is 71% water. The human body is closer to 80% water. Both dry up and die without water. Water is essential for helping plants and trees to survive. Likewise without water, we dry up and become dysfunctional. I could continue but I am sure you are getting the message. Water is absolutely essential to every facet of life. I remember the days when I pastored a church in the UK. I used to preach every Sunday. I preached long and hard. When I was finished my delivery, I did not want orange juice, tea or any other beverages. I just could not wait to get my hands on a bottle of ice cold water. I would down those ice cold bottles one after the other. It seems to me there is a thirst that only the pure, transparent, God like purity of water will quench.

My love for water extends beyond consumption of it as some years ago I taught myself to swim. I find water the most perfect place in which to meditate upon and hear from God. Over the years I have also noticed that I have had some of my most tremendous revelations of the word of God whilst in the shower! Someone once said that cleanliness is next to godliness. There may be some truth in that although I am not sure of the origin of the statement.

So why is Jesus like water?

Firstly because like water, we cannot live without Him. Some of us think we can but without Him we simply die. This is why the Bible says "In Him was life and that life is the light of men". There are millions of people on planet earth today who do not know Jesus and consequently are dying every day bereft of His amazing life and love. Secondly, the Bible is literally gushing with revelation about the letter Mem being a picture of Christ. We will be looking at a number of verses in order to cover Mem efficiently so you will need your Bible handy.

The Bible says there are three witnesses in the earth which agree. These are the Spirit, the water and the blood. (1John 5:8). We know about the Holy Spirit. We studied his blood in the first letter Aleph. Now let us take a close look at some scriptures where Christ declares His relationship to water. Firstly, The prophet Jeremiah's declaration

"Blessed is the man who trusts in the Lord, and whose hope is the Lord. For he shall be like a tree planted by the waters, which spreads out its roots by the river, And will not fear when heat comes; but its leaf will be green, and will not be anxious in the year of drought, nor will cease from yielding fruit". Jeremiah 17 : 7-8

Child of God, tribulations and trials will come, but the one who puts first his trust in God will not fear or become unfruitful. Let us also examine some of David's thoughts in the Psalms.

"Blessed is the man, who walks not in the counsel of the ungodly, nor stands in the path of sinners, nor sits in the seat of the scornful; But his delight is in the law of the Lord, and in His law he meditates day and night. He shall be like a tree planted by the rivers of water, that brings forth its fruit in its season", Psalm 1:1-3

Notice the connection with the word meditation, which he writes of here and then connects it to water. He does this also in verse 99 of the current stanza about Mem. I believe he is speaking about a kind of total saturation in the word of God that only comes from spending deep times literally immersed in the word, hence the connection to water. Note also prior to this, in verse 98, he records the word of God is ever with him. I remember years ago hearing a story about the great British Apostle of the faith, Smith Wigglesworth. Someone once asked him for the secret of his great power. He answered "The power comes from spending time in prayer". The young inquisitive man continued; "Well how long do you pray?" He said "Oh about five minutes each time". "Five minutes!" The young man exclaimed! "Yes", said Smith, "But there are never more than five minutes between every prayer". Like Mem, This is a picture of total immersion in the word of God. Now we go to the Prophet Isaiah, who paints for us an allegory which is undeniably a picture of Christ.

"For as the rain comes down, and the snow from heaven, and do not return there, But water the earth, and make it bring forth and bud, that it may give seed to the sower And bread to the eater. So shall My word be that goes forth from My mouth; It shall not return to Me void, But it shall accomplish what I please, And it shall prosper in the thing for which I sent it.
Isaiah 55 : 10 - 11.

The aforementioned verses are the almighty God speaking through the great prophet. It is the first and ONLY time that God will describe Himself in allegorical terms. What is the picture He draws? Pure H20. Water has the ability to fill every nook of any vessel it is poured into. Likewise, the word of God will find its way to every corner of our planet. He says My word will be like rain water falling to the earth, forcing it to bring forth fruit. The Hebrew for bringing forth, is a term that is used for a midwife, "Yawlad". This term is used twice here, Yawlad, Yawlad, meaning that Jesus (The word) will bring about the new birth of the spirit with unending fruitfulness. He will bring forth and bring forth forever without end. Amen! God said that His word will not return void unto Him but it will accomplish what He pleased. Do you remember the final words of Christ from the cross of Calvary? "It is finished." And with these words, He bowed his head and gave up His spirit. He had accomplished the task. God's word is about to bear fruit in its season. Selah. The Bible declares that with two or three witness, the truth is established.

We have heard Jeremiah, David and Isaiah. Now let us go to the Christ Himself. When we studied Yod, we talked about the declaration that Christ made openly at the height of the great feast.

On the last day, that great day of the feast, Jesus stood and cried out, saying, "If anyone thirsts, let him come to Me and drink. He who believes in Me, as the Scripture has said, out of his heart will flow rivers of living water." John 7: 37-38

And finally then to the woman of Samaria, at the well.

Jesus answered and said to her, "If you knew the gift of God, and who it is who says to you, 'Give Me a drink,' you would have asked Him, and He would have given you living water." John 4:10

Yes! Christ identifies Himself openly as water. When we receive Him, we receive the washing of water by the word. We could go on and on but there is no need. Suffice to say, when you see water in scripture, you are seeing picture of Christ.

I would like to finish Mem with one final thought. It has to do with the purity of water and a connection with healing. Take a look at the following scripture:

"So you shall serve the Lord your God, and He will bless your bread and your water. And I will take sickness away from the midst of you". Exodus 23:25

I would like you to see a trinity contained here in these words. The servant. The Lord your God, and "I". Can you see that? Who is the "I" speaking? Well it certainly isn't the writer Moses. I believe the Lord had him scribe these words exactly this way, not so much for the benefit of the children of Israel, (although they would have benefited from it). It was written more for the sake of the church of the living God today. The "I" is alluding to the Holy Spirit. There have been times when I was sick. I would take a glass of pure water and declare it blessed of God based on this scripture. There is nothing added by man. My glass isn't holier than yours. I did not buy it from a ministry claiming to have blessed it for me. It was not drawn from a grotto where Mary prayed. It isn't ionised with salt from the river Jordan in Israel. It is simply my water. I poured it from my own bottle. It became mine when I paid for it. What am I getting at? I would drink that water by faith and often times I would quickly receive my healing. Why? Because I believed the word of God and received what it said by faith. Fresh water is the purest of substances on earth, untouched by the hand of man, so no man on earth can get the credit for your healing. With these words we close another beautiful stanza.

In conclusion. As in the case of baptism, Mem reminds us of the complete and wonderful benefits of total immersion in the word of the living God and that Christ Himself is the source of our living water. As water compasses our bodies and the earth likewise the Word surrounds us!

The MEM Prayer

Heavenly Father, help us to be so hungry for more of your word that we seek instruction, knowledge and revelation from your word daily. We want to be filled with all the fullness of you and what you have for us and others. As water fills the earth and all life, so also let us be filled to overflowing.

Amen

The Fourteenth Letter

NUN

CHAPTER 14

NUN
The Fish or Whale

Your word is a lamp to my feet And a light to my path.
I have sworn and confirmed that I will keep Your righteous
judgments. I am afflicted very much;
Revive me, O Lord, according to Your word.
Accept, I pray, the freewill offerings of my mouth, O Lord, And
teach me Your judgments. My life is continually in my hand, Yet
I do not forget Your law.
The wicked have laid a snare for me,
Yet I have not strayed from Your precepts.
Your testimonies I have taken as a heritage forever,
For they are the rejoicing of my heart.
I have inclined my heart to perform Your statutes
Forever, to the very end.

Psalms 119 : 105 -112

Jesus the Aleph Tav

NUN is symbolic of the fish which speaks of productiveness and increase. We know it was first drawn as a fish. It is also rumoured that the tradition of drawing it may have continued during the time of Christ.

Around about 64AD, as Christianity began to grow, believers were horribly targeted for persecution as a group by the emperor Nero. Christians could no longer meet openly, so they met in secret to share the word and fellowship. Scholars of Christianity's history tell of a secret code that was used by believers during this time. The fledgeling church became aware that Nero was planting spies within the community to pose as Christians in order to destroy them. So, upon meeting another suspected believer for the first time, legend has it that a group of Christians created a code to catch Nero out in his plans. Upon meeting a believer for the first time half a fish would be surreptitiously drawn in the sand or dirt. If the other person was a believer, they would complete the drawing. Although I cannot prove that this actually happened, a little experiment with the letter Nun does illustrate that it could have been likely. I say this especially because the early church was largely made up of Jewish believers. Note the following image where I have doubled and flipped the letter Nun. It does look somewhat like a stylised fish.

This letter has a certain personal significance for this writer. Any who are familiar with my ministry will know that over the years I have been guided very much by dreams and visions. At some point in the late 90s I had a dream in which someone took me to the rooftop of the house and said the following words to me. "This house is called Yebule". I sensed it was Jesus so I went to see my Pastor at the time, to tell him what I had seen. We sat and prayed together about it but he could not imagine what it meant. This was the early days of the internet so we searched for it also. Eventually, I put it to the back of my mind and forgot about it. Years later we were having a Bible study at our home group. I needed to check the Hebrew definition of another word. After finding the word in my Strongs Hebrew Dictionary, I heard a voice inside saying "Look for Yebule". I thumbed just a few pages on and whoa! There it was! Yebule! The definition was to be fruitful and increase.

You know it's amazing to me today, that it took me two years to find out the meaning of that dream. This was purely because I had no concept of the Jewishness of Jesus Christ. If I had known then what I know today, I would have gone straight to my Strongs and had the answer. God chose to speak to me, a young Christian believer, in Hebrew because He knew it was part of my calling to do what I am doing today. To preach not just Christianity, but to preach the complete Judeo Christian Gospel. He was telling me that If I would devote my house to this cause, He would add the increase!

Nun teaches us that when Christ comes into your life, He brings His fruitfulness and His increase along with Him. A believer who is able to receive this by faith will experience the increase of God in his or her life.

Other associations between NUN and Christ

Jesus spent much of his young life on the shores of the river Galilee. Places like Capernaum were renowned for being fishing villages. Remember when the Christ called Peter to the ministry? He told Jesus he had caught no fish after toiling all night. Jesus told to try again casting his net into the deep on the other side. He caught a BOATLOAD of fish and his boat nearly sank! In fact he caught so many fish they had to call other boats to help! That is what i call increase!

Jesus said to Peter from now on you will catch men rather than fish. Increase! When we meet with Jesus, everything is on the increase! Another illustration of increase is also found in the book of John.

"Most assuredly, I say to you, unless a grain of wheat falls into the ground and dies, it remains alone; but if it dies, it produces much grain". John 12:24.

Christ is the seed of increase! And you and I are a part of the great harvest.

Joshua, one of the greatest heroes of the Old Testament, shares two points of significance here. Firstly, Joshua is a derivative of Yeshua (Jesus). Both names mean exactly the same thing. He will bring salvation. Secondly, The Bible tells us that Joshua came from the family of Nun. This letter unlocks a mystery concerning why Moses did not lead the children of Israel into the promised land. According to Jewish midrash (historical canon) "The son of him whose name was as the name of a fish would lead them [the Israelites] into the land".

The letter Nun also points us to a significant prophetic picture by symbolising the fish. That picture of course is the account of Jonah. Jesus Himself makes this comparison in the book of Matthew.

"As Jonah was three days and three nights in the belly of the great fish, so will the Son of Man be three days and three nights in the heart of the earth" . Matthew 12 :40

Nun reminds us that the Lord indeed spent three days and three nights in the heart of the earth after Calvary. In the first chapter of Revelation, Christ Jesus introduces Himself with the following words;

"I am He who lives, and was dead, and behold, I am alive forevermore Revelation 1:18".

Glory to God! Jesus is saying I was alive in the earth, I died there. Then I rose from the dead and now I am alive forevermore. 1 Peter 3:19 then tells us that Christ went somewhere to preach to the spirits who were in prison. Nun reminds us exactly where He went. As Jonah was in the great fish, so Christ was in the heart of the earth. I believe when Jesus breathed His last earthly breath, His Spirit left His body and appeared in hell. This was because He was carrying all of the sin of mankind on His shoulders. Take a moment to think about that. If any person leaves earth still carrying the burden of sin, they have only one destiny. The heart of the earth. The sad truth is, unsaved people drop immediately into darkness, as if a weight is tied around their feet. This is so sad because Jesus Christ died for all of our sins. He does not want any to perish but rather that all will know eternal life with Him. Jesus turned up in eternal darkness and all of a sudden the place was filled with light. Death and hell was in a state of confusion. The Bible says none of the princes, (demonic powers) of this world knew what was going to happen otherwise they would not have crucified the Lord of Glory. (1Cor 2:8). They did, and Christ emerged victorious with the keys of death and hades in His hands.

We used to sing a wonderful song in my first church it went;

"My soul magnifies the Lord, And my spirit praises His name
Even death could not Hold him captive, Even in the grave,
He is Lord".

In conclusion Nun reminds us that the Word of God is always making us fruitful. We clearly see its ability to cause us to increase in every way. Nun also points us to Christ's victory over the grave through a depiction of Jonah who, although swallowed by the great fish, survived to preach the Gospel. Nun tells us that Christ went to hell for our sakes but He did not stay there because death could not hold Him. Darkness cannot hold light. Even in the grave, He is Lord. Hallelujah!

The NUN Prayer

Thank you Lord for we know your intentions towards us are perfect. Your presence in our lives produces increase, fruit, wealth and happiness. Help us to accept your kindness and grace even when we feel that we do not deserve it. As we increase in blessings from you, let it be for the good of the Kingdom of God as well as our lives.

Amen

The Fifteenth Letter

SAMEK

Jesus the Aleph Tav

CHAPTER 15

SAMEK
The Prop or Support

I hate the double-minded, But I love Your law.
You are my hiding place and my shield; I hope in Your
word. Depart from me, you evildoers, For I will keep the
commandments of my God!
Uphold me according to Your word, that I may live;
And do not let me be ashamed of my hope. Hold me up, and I
shall be safe, And I shall observe Your statutes continually. You
reject all those who stray from Your statutes,
For their deceit is falsehood.
You put away all the wicked of the earth like dross;
Therefore I love Your testimonies.
My flesh trembles for fear of You,
And I am afraid of Your judgments.

Psalms 119 : 113 - 120

We have seen so many wonderful allegories of God's word and of Jesus Christ that when we reach the 15th letter it is almost hard to believe that there is still so much more revelation to be gained. Believe me, there is much, much more! As we were researching these truths I kept saying "Lord is there yet more?" There always was...

In terms of depth of revelation and beauty, Samek does not disappoint. Samek is symbolic of a prop or support. It speaks to us of the absolute surety of God's word. It reminds us of the absolute reliability of God's promises and of His unfailing strength in our lives.

Perhaps you are sitting as you read this book. Years ago we had a house with a very big garden. We bought some green lawn furniture which was on sale. The first time I sat in one of those green chairs, I was shocked by how unstable it was. They were made of cheap plastic and the legs would bend very easily. Every time I sat in that chair I had a fear that I would fall off it. One day my fear was realised, I sat on the chair, the leg broke and I went tumbling to the ground. That was the last time that we bought cheap garden furniture. When you sat down on your chair or sofa to read this book, you had complete confidence that it would support you. This is a picture of Samek. It illustrates the inner knowing that God's word is dependable, reliable and always a surety in our lives. Samek says "If the

Lord said it then that's the end of it. Do not question it".

As you have read through some of these definitions, you may have thought as I did, that the Hebrew letters were possibly added later by translators. I.e., Not actually included by David at the time of writing. Perhaps somebody noticed that there were 22 stanzas, and decided to match them to the Hebrew letters. It is a fair point. Sometimes translators did add colour to the scriptures to illustrate a point but in most study Bibles, those words are italicised so that we would know they were not part of the original text. In this case Samek really confirms to us that the letters were there at the time of writing. Indeed I believe the Holy Spirit inspired David to write each stanza with a clear understanding of its pictorial reference and meaning. Let us walk with David through some keys within the stanza. Together we shall unpack what David could have meant at the time of writing. He begins by saying "I hate the double minded but I love your law". Double minded people are unstable but God's word is solid. In verse 116 he says "Uphold me according to your word that I may live" . Again David is sharing with us a revelation that he cannot live without God's support in his life.

There have been so many times in my own life, where I have had exactly the same sentiment. I truly do not know how I would still be alive if God had not been there upholding me.

Again, David says "Uphold me according to your word". We should not miss this. He is not asking for a physical upholding at that point. David was a King. He had enough people to hold him physically. He is asking God to allow His word to do the upholding because he is absolutely sure of the validity and reliability of God's word. Glory hallelujah!

In verse 117 he says "Hold me up and I shall be safe". When my daughter was a small baby just learning how to walk I would sometimes take her out to a small park. If she saw something that worried her she would cry and I would immediately lift her up. I would point to whatever it was that scared her. A cat, a dog a funny looking flower. I would say it is okay baby girl, Daddy's got you. As long as you are with me you have got nothing to be afraid about. That little dog or cat cannot do you any harm. She was completely happy and at peace because her daddy was holding her in his arms. I think this is what David is illustrating here. Jesus Christ said that it was necessary for us to enter the Kingdom of God as children. I believe we need to be able to hold up our arms to the Father and be able to say Daddy I am scared.

Sometimes as believers we need to hear God the Father say "Do not worry son or daughter as long as you're with me, you have got nothing to be afraid about ". Isn't that beautiful? Proverbs chapter 3 says;

'Trust in the Lord with all of your heart and lean not on your own understanding in all of your ways acknowledge him and he shall direct your path's' . Proverbs 3:5

Notice the scripture says that we should not lean on our own understanding. I think this is a very important point because it is our own understanding that often will cause us to miss the Lord's perfect purpose in our lives. We must learn to lean on His wisdom especially when we are fighting diverse battles pertaining to our daily lives. Perhaps you are facing horrible circumstances in your life presently. You may have tried every possible way to work your problem out. However, it just will not go away. I know how that feels. I know what it feels like to be desperate and destitute. Perhaps your problem may be physical. Perhaps it may be financial or even mental. You might be depressed or lonely. You might be sad or frightened or even suicidal. Whatever you may be going through, allow this little Hebrew letter to speak to your heart right now. Allow it to tell you that Jesus is fully aware of what you're going through. Stop trying to work it out for yourself and lean on Him.

We will end Samek with some powerful words from the Apostle Paul.

'Be anxious for nothing,
but in everything by prayer and supplication,
with thanksgiving, let your requests be made known to God;
and the peace of God,
which surpasses all understanding,
will guard your hearts and minds
through Christ Jesus' Phil 4: 6 - 7

In conclusion; Samek represents the prop or support. It reminds us that without God we simply cannot stand and that He will be our strength and support when we are about to fall. And that those who trust in Jesus lean not in their own understanding.

The Samek Prayer

According to Proverbs 3:5 we trust you with all of our heart and lean on you instead of our own understanding. We hereby acknowledge you in all of our ways, trusting that you will always direct our paths. We thank you for this precious promise in your word which declares that without you we cannot stand.

Amen

The Sixteenth Letter

AYIN

Jesus the Aleph Tav

CHAPTER 16

AYIN
The Eye of the Lord

*I have done justice and righteousness; Do not leave me to my
oppressors. Be surety for Your servant for good; Do not let the
proud oppress me. My eyes fail from seeking Your salvation
And Your righteous word. Deal with Your servant according to
Your mercy, And teach me Your statutes.
I am Your servant; Give me understanding,
That I may know Your testimonies.
It is time for You to act, O Lord,
For they have regarded Your law as void.
Therefore I love Your commandments
More than gold, yes, than fine gold!
Therefore all Your precepts concerning all things
I consider to be right; I hate every false way.*

Psalms 119 : 121 - 128

Ayin is the second Hebrew letter which has no equivalent sound in the English language. It sounds like a choke or a gargle. There is a complete list of alpha equivalences in the glossary section at the back of the book.

You can almost visualise this letter being drawn as a hieroglyphic image in a cave somewhere. Ayin looks like a perfectly drawn a human eye seen from a side angle. It took me some time to see it at first. The sense we get from it is that it speaks either of seeing or the ability to see. It also has another beautiful connotation. It is sometimes defined as a fountain.

Ayin is multi dimensional. Firstly, in terms of relationship, there are two perspectives. Ours and God's. In addition to these, there are also multiple perceptions to consider. These could be described as natural, super natural and divine eyesight. Equally, we have the idea of gaining understanding, by becoming enlightened.

"The lamp of the body is the eye. If therefore your eye is good, your whole body will be full of light. But if your eye is bad, your whole body will be full of darkness. If therefore the light that is in you is darkness, how great is that darkness!" Matthew 6:22-23

If we carefully de-construct these words, Christ is actually teaching us two amazing things. Firstly, we find that the eye is the lamp or illumination of the body.

That is like saying my headlamps are the illumination of the road ahead when I am driving my car. Let us break this thought down a little bit further for a moment. The only way for light to enter the body is through the eye. In the same way, the only way for God's power to enter this world is through His word. (The Christ, the Word of God) If therefore we continue removing the word of God from our schools, our governments, our thinking and our legislation, light cannot enter! Well you say, suppose a person is blind? Is this unfortunate person simply bound for hell, just because he was born this way? No! Because a blind person can still hear through audio or even read the word of God through touch using the Braille system.

Sight is so precious to those who can see but not to a person who has never known the faculty. During an Interview, the performer Ray Charles was once asked a hyperthetical question. "If there was ever a cure discovered for blindless, would he choose to have his sight restored by modern science"? His response was *"If possible, I would take it for a day and then they put me back as I am. I would just like to see what my children look like. I am not interested in much else".*

Now I do not know about you, but the fact that a blind person could experience the world in such a satisfied manner that he would dismiss the idea of regaining sight, makes my mind boggle. It seems to me that sight is so very important to every human being. However, God is merciful and kind so He gives ability to those without sight, to perceive the world in ways that we cannot.

Some years ago, the Lord blessed me with a great experience. I fell asleep on my sofa one day, then suddenly I was caught up in a fantastic vision. I found myself far above the earth, somewhere in the Heavens above. As I looked down I saw a round building with a hole in the top. I immediately perceived that it was a church. The people inside the church were worshipping God. I saw, as it were, a flower. Not an ordinary flower but a living flower (moving with the actions of a swimming fish) emerging from the hole in the top of the church. It was a fire coloured Rose. I watched it as it sped towards where I was located in the Heavens. Suddenly I knew that I was perceiving worship the way God receives it. The rose became bigger and bigger until it was larger than the Earth, then it exploded into what seemed like a billion particles which seemed to pass straight through me. It literally took my breath away. I was both frightened and elated simultaneously.

How do I put my experience into words? I did not taste it, or feel it, I could not smell it, hear it, or see it. I experienced this rose of worship in a way that I am presently unable to explain. I suppose I understand what people mean when they talk about a sixth sense, I certainly experienced one that day. Having experienced this, who knows how a blind person perceives the world?

The second thing He is teaching us is absolutely revelatory. The Christ is saying that it is possible to be illuminated by both light or darkness. We understand that in all cases light will always prevail over darkness. A torch will allow you to see in the dark but darkness still surrounds the beam of light. Darkness is ever imposing its presence where light is absent. In this case, Christ is saying that it is possible to be "illuminated" by darkness. As in the case of Adam and Eve.

'Then the eyes (Ayin) of both of them were opened, and they knew that they were naked; and they sewed fig leaves together and made themselves coverings'. Genesis 3:7

Before the fall, the couple had perfect 'divine eyesight'. God warned Adam not to partake of the fruit in the midst of the garden because the result would be death. Notice that after they disobeyed God, their eyes were open. The Hebrew word for this is "paqah", meaning "to open the senses, especially the eyes". They were enlightened or illuminated, not by light, but instead by sin. Take a moment to think about that. There is a reason why so many of us fall into temptation. It is because sin seems to be so attractive. Its doctrines are sensual and addictive to the human condition (The flesh). For a fleeting moment, sin felt great to them. After all, where would temptation be without the resulting pleasure? Readers please be warned. Like Adam and Eve, our AYIN could be opened to darkness as well or instead of light.

Jesus is saying that if your source of enlightenment is dark, (wicked, evil, satanic, demonic or even secular humanist) darkness will fill your entire being. Darkness can take you over if you let it in. And then, how great that darkness will become with the absence of light.

" There is a way which seems right to a man and appears straight before him, but at the end of it is the way of death ".
Proverbs 14:12 Amplified.

Our eyes are the gateway to the soul. They are the gateway for both light and darkness. Fellow children of God, Ayin reminds us that we must guard our "eye gates", if we want our bodies to remain filled with light. Amen.

In the book of 2nd Kings we find an amazing account. It tells of a certain King of Syria who made war against the children of Israel. He planned ambush after ambush but the Lord had opened the Ayin of a certain prophet named Elisha, who repeatedly warned the King of Israel. Eventually the King of Syria sent a huge ambush for Elisha, whose servants brought him a terrifying report.

And when the servant of the man of God arose early and went out, there was an army, surrounding the city with horses and chariots. And his servant said to him, "Alas, my master! What shall we do?"

So he answered, "Do not fear, for those who are with us are more than those who are with them." And Elisha prayed, and said, "Lord, I pray, open his eyes that he may see." Then the Lord opened the eyes of the young man, and he saw.

And behold, the mountain was full of horses and chariots of fire all around Elisha. 2 Kings 6 15-17

The word for 'eyes' used in this scripture is Ayin. The text is showing us that God is able to open up our Ayin so that we can see into the spirit realm. In fact, whenever a Christian experiences a vision, it is always because God has opened their Ayin. I simply call this divine eyesight which God will allow many of us to experience in our earthly walk. One whose Ayin has been specially opened might be called a "SEER". This is slightly distinct to a Prophet although they are often used interchangeably. For example; although I have been known to give prophecies, I do not operate in the office of a Prophet at all times. On the other hand, the ministry calling that appears to be permanently switched on in my life, is the office of the SEER. As a matter of fact, the Lord actually appeared to me in a vision and told me this was my calling and office. I simply see what He wants me to see and share it. The hardest part for people like me, is learning how and when to express what we see. It might take a lifetime to develop that wisdom.

I mentioned earlier that Ayin can also be defined as a fountain. What a perfect description for this beautiful part of the body which gives away so much of our emotions. We cry when we are happy. We cry when we are sad. This fountain opens up and pours out the state of our hearts for all to see. Is not that a beautiful thought? Someone once wrote that the eyes are the window to the soul. Perhaps it would be more accurate to say the eyes are a window from the soul. I wish this was not the case sometimes, especially when we are watching sad movies. My eyes just give it all away. I am a BIG softy! As you can see, AYIN is like an onion skin with many layers of revelation.

God's Perspective.

'For the eyes of the Lord run to and fro throughout the whole earth, to show Himself strong on behalf of those whose heart is loyal (Perfect) to Him' . (2 Chronicles 16:9)

The aforementioned allows us to see Ayin from God's perspective. Note how in this scripture, the Ayin refers to the "eyes of the Lord". We can see them scanning planet earth for that one whose heart is perfected towards Him. God is alive my friends! He is aware of everything that we do. He is watching from Heaven. He is watching through Angels. He is watching through the eyes of the Holy Spirit. God sees everything. There is no hiding from Him. Selah!

'Where can I go from Your Spirit? Or where can I flee from Your presence? ' (Psalm 139 :7)

How many times have we had the following thoughts: Is God really there for me? Is the Almighty actually aware of what is going on in my life? Are His eyes truly watching over me? I want to tell you in closing, that He is. No matter how you may feel, God is actually watching over you. Please receive this in your spirit man or woman now. If you have received Jesus, His eye is upon you.

If you haven't received him, do not worry there is time. Why not repent of any darkness that may be in your life now. Ask Him into your heart. Ask Him to be your Lord and to forgive all of your sin. If you ask Him with a genuine heart, He will. No matter how dark you may consider your life to be. His light will overcome.

'The eyes of the Lord are on the righteous, And His ears are open to their cry' . Psalm 34:15

Jesus said His eye is on the Sparrow and you are of much more value than that beautiful little bird.

David's View

Now what about David's perspective on Ayin? The stanza is filled with references to the eye or illumination. In verse 123 he says; 'My eyes fail from seeking Your salvation' (natural vision). This is a direct reference to Ayin. Also in verse 125, he asks for understanding. This, as we said before, is a synonym of light entering the eye (Divine enlightenment). He finally says he loves the commandments of God more than fine gold. I believe he says this because gold is a visual enhancer. People wear gold because they believe it looks great. Remember, he was a King and as such would have seen a lot of gold.   David is saying;

as beautiful as Gold may be, I would rather look at your word. He does not stop there. Ayin's alternative meaning purposely finds its way into the next stanza also which will become clear as we review the next chapter.

I have done my best to pour out what I have been shown. I now trust the Lord to open your Ayin to the full revelation of this beautiful Hebrew letter. In conclusion Ayin teaches us so very much, it is difficult to actually bring the chapter to a conclusion. However, the key points are: Ayin teaches us that the word of God is the entry point of all illumination. God's light comes through the Lord Jesus Christ and His Word. Ayin warns us to watch over our eyes. Be careful what we take in through them.

Ayin also reminds us that those who walk with Christ, walk in the light of God's wisdom and truth.

There is so much more that we could say about this beautiful Hebrew letter but we have the complete Aleph Tav to go through. I am sure the Lord will open your understanding to see the height width and depth of whatever remains unsaid pertaining to this chapter. God bless you as you continue our study.

The Ayin Prayer

Lord open our eyes that we may see the truth in your word. Allow us to see what you want us to see and for your word to discern and help us when we are in need. As your eyes survey the earth, you see us for who we truly are. May we see you for who you truly are also.

Amen

The Seventeenth Letter

PE

Jesus the Aleph Tav

CHAPTER 17

PE
The Mouth or Tongue

Your testimonies are wonderful; Therefore my soul keeps them. The entrance of Your words gives light; It gives understanding to the simple. I opened my mouth and panted, For I longed for Your commandments.
Look upon me and be merciful to me, As Your custom is toward those who love Your name. Direct my steps by Your word, And let no iniquity have dominion over me. Redeem me from the oppression of man, that I may keep Your precepts.
Make Your face shine upon Your servant, And teach me Your statutes. Rivers of water run down from my eyes, Because men do not keep Your law.

Psalms 119 : 129 - 136

Pe is without a doubt, another letter that carries the most incredible significance for me personally. It is multi dimensional and full of revelation and power. On this occasion we will begin with thoughts from the stanza. David seems to continue his thoughts concerning Ayin directly into the stanza for Pe. If you read his intent, it is almost as if the two letters are one. He even closes with the words;

Rivers of water run down from my eyes, (Ayin)
Because men do not keep Your law.

I do not believe this is co-incidental. Pe is the mouth so immediately we see a connection. Firstly, both the eye and the mouth are facial elements. The face is the part of the body which engages with the rest of the world. Secondly, Jesus said "it is not what enters a man that makes him unclean but rather what comes out of him". Through these two factors, we can now understand that the eye and the mouth are both "gate ways". David is helping us to understand that whatever we studiously take in our eyes, will be reflected from our mouths.

David begins this stanza with some of the most profound words ever scribed in scripture. He says the entrance of your words brings light.. Again, through the words of Jesus Christ we can see the connection with the last letter clearly.

Pe deserves an entire book of its own. This letter is about the organ which brings forth words. It is through the spoken word that man enjoys his closest relationship with God the Father. Why? Because everything that God created began with His spoken word. Whenever God wants to create anything, He always begins with His word. Words are therefore the most important facet of creation especially in the Holy Bible because Jesus Himself is the Word.

When we began to research the letter Pe, something extraordinary happened. We had not had very much time to research the letter in time for the impending broadcast, so we sat down to pray together. Within seconds of doing so I had a vision of a donkey! Its mouth appeared to be moving as though it was speaking. I knew there was an account in the Bible of a donkey that spoke so we went there immediately to ascertain the Lord's direction. There, in the book of Numbers chapter 22 we found the account of two men named Balak and Balaam.

The children of Israel at this point had not yet come to rest in their own land. They were still a transient people searching for the promised land. Their journey brought them to the plains of Moab. The Children of Israel were at that time, very much feared in the region. Primarily because of the number of them but also because they had completely destroyed all of the Amorites who had previously opposed them. At that time, Balak was the king of the Moabites. He sent messages to Balaam requesting that he would come and place a curse on the people of Israel. Now Balaam was not an Israelite yet we understand from scripture that he had some prophetic abilities. Balaam could be described as a practiser of divination. God, who clearly has some kind of relationship with Balaam, visited him in the night and told him to go with the princes of Moab but only to speak what He tells him to speak.

(Authors note: Here we see God in dialogue with a bad man. As in the case of Lucifer, the Jewish Talmud teaches the Balaam began life as a prophet, but he became evil and was later demoted and called a diviner who finally perishes by the sword.)

The next morning as Balaam began his journey, the Bible says that God's anger was aroused. This would have been because Balaam was planning to follow the instructions of Balak instead of doing what God had said. Also later in the chapter, God said Balaam's way was perverse.   The Lord God sent an angel to block Balaam's way three times but he could not see him. The innocent donkey on the other hand could.

Every time the donkey saw the Angel of the Lord, he tried to turn back or run away. Balaam had no idea what was happening so he just kept beating that poor old donkey until eventually this happens.

Then the Lord opened the mouth of the donkey, and she said to Balaam, "What have I done to you, that you have struck me these three times?"

And Balaam said to the donkey, "Because you have abused me. I wish there were a sword in my hand, for now I would kill you!"

So the donkey said to Balaam, "Am I not your donkey on which you have ridden, ever since I became yours, to this day? Was I ever disposed to do this to you?"

And he said, "No."

Then the Lord opened Balaam's eyes, and he saw the Angel of the Lord standing in the way with His drawn sword in His hand; and he bowed his head and fell flat on his face
Numbers 22 : 28-31

The account has a fascinating ending. Balaam is unable to curse Israel after that. In fact he ends up blessing them.

As marvellous as the story is, the focus is not on Balak or Balaam but on the lowly simple donkey, which God showed me. Balaam was supposed to be a Prophet of God yet we are shown that even the lowly donkey had more discernment than him. This is apparent but I believe God gave me this vision because He wanted us to understand something else quite unique about the letter Pe.

As I said earlier Pe speaks of the mouth. Not an ordinary mouth, but rather a mouth that has been opened divinely and supernaturally by God. The illustration of the donkey is very profound. Why? Because donkeys unlike human beings and possibly parrots, have no natural faculty of speech. Everything therefore, that the donkey spoke, must have been divinely placed in his mouth (Pe) by God. Pe therefore, speaks profoundly to us of the believer in Christ having the ability to speak divine words of utterance as God permits.

Christians, through these words, have power to alter adverse circumstances in both their own and in other peoples lives. This is not a matter to be taken lightly, because words are the very substance of creation. The elements are held together by the power of God's word. In the same way, the very elements of our lives may be affected and changed by the power of our words. When mature Christians speak Gods word, just like our Father's words, they will not return unto us void but they will accomplish what He pleases in our lives. My friends, do not be afraid to think this way! You are a child of God. As fathers, we want our children to inherit the best of who we are. likewise, God wants His children to emulate the best of him.

The letter Pe also has a secondary meaning. It means an edge. Specifically a sharp edge. This immediately brings several scriptural thoughts to mind. We have already discussed the 7th letter Zayin, the sword of the Lord. Do you see how these letters overlap creating a wonderful pastiche of truth. We can now understand that God wants to give His children the edge in this world through the sword of the Spirit, which His Holy word.

At this point, I must again pay a debt of homage to my Lord. He was and is the greatest teacher that ever walked on planet earth. This is none other than Jesus Christ Himself. Please observe his teaching found in the book of Mark chapter 11.

"Have faith in God. For assuredly, I say to you, whoever says to this mountain, 'Be removed and be cast into the sea,' and does not doubt in his heart, but believes that those things he says will be done, he will have whatever he says. Therefore I say to you, whatever things you ask when you pray, believe that you receive them, and you will have them". Mark 11 : 23-24

Now that we understand Pe, perhaps it will be easier for us to understand why the Lord has such incredible faith in His creation. You see, God knows and understands the power of the words that we carry. May God open our "Pe" today!

The aforementioned words of Christ were not collections of allegorical hyper thesis. These are absolute truths! Many of His revelations are far too high for us to grasp presently. It remains my belief however, that one day, somewhere on planet earth, someone will muster enough faith in the words of Jesus Christ to stand before a mountain and speak with the rumble of the earth following. Is this really so hard to believe? After all we read in the book of Joshua what happened when he needed more daylight time to destroy his enemy.

'Then Joshua spoke to the Lord in the day when the Lord delivered up the Amorites before the children of Israel, and he said in the sight of Israel: "Sun, stand still over Gibeon; And Moon, in the Valley of Aijalon." So the sun stood still, And the moon stopped,' Joshua 10 :12-13

The Bible also records a time when the people of Israel collectively shouted. The shout was so loud and so powerful that the very earth itself reverberated! (1Samuel 4:5). The planet shook not because of the volume of the shout but rather because of the power within that shout. The Bible in Leviticus 26:8 says "Five of you shall chase a hundred, and a hundred of you shall put ten thousand to flight your enemies shall fall by the sword before you".

Imagine what we could do as Christians if we could pull

together and use our collective shout? My mind certainly boggles at the thought. Now note the amazing reaction from the people who saw the power of the words spoken by Jesus when He cast a demon out. Pay attention to the profound way in which their words bring (Pe) into focus.

'Then they were all amazed and spoke among themselves, saying, "WHAT A WORD THIS IS! For with authority and power He commands the unclean spirits, and they come out." And the report about Him went out into every place in the surrounding region'. Luke 4:36-37

They could have said "What a man is this?" Yet they did not. Their cry instead is "WHAT A WORD IS THIS?" With these words, they are bringing direct attention to the Word of God.

Finally, I would like to explore one more thought about Pe. A careful study of the Bible reveals another wonderful truth for us. There is a relationship between divinely spoken words (spoken from the Pe) and angels. They listen to and respond to our words spoken from our mouths (Pe).

"Bless the Lord, you His angels, Who excel in strength, who do His word, Heeding the voice of His word." Psalm 103:20

In the book of Daniel, an angel turns up to answer Daniel's prayer. His first words were;

"Do not fear, Daniel, for from the first day that you set your heart to understand, and to humble yourself before your God, your words were heard; and I have come because of your words". Daniel 10:12

Yes my friends, Angels indeed hearken to the word of God. Since we are part of the body of Christ, washed in his blood. We, through the Holy Spirit have been given authority to speak in the earth, like the Lord Jesus did. I sense that some people may be offended by these words. Some will say that no man can speak like God. In this sentiment I agree with them. In fact, I completely emphasise with their intention to honour God. However, I would ask such dear brothers and sisters in Christ to consider the following. God opened the mouth (Pe) of a donkey allowing him to speak divine words. How much more likely do you think it would be that God would open the mouth of one of His sons or daughters? In this regard, God uses the lowly donkey's open mouth to close ours.

I would like to end this session with a warning from the word of the Lord.

"Death and life are in the power of the tongue, and those who love it will eat its fruit". Proverbs 18 : 21

Pe teaches us that as Christians we must learn how and when to speak. We must also learn when and what not to speak. I am afraid that many of us fall victim to our very own spoken words because we have not heeded the many warnings from scripture. Notice, this Proverb places the word death before the word life. This is because human beings are in a fallen state. Our propensity is to speak death rather than life. This undoubtedly is the reason for the unusual reversal. We must try our very best not to be like Job, who according to the Bible opened his mouth (Pe) and cursed his own day. (Job 3:1)

In Conclusion, Pe really is a most empowering Hebrew letter. It brings to us that factor of Christ's life which demolishes all the work of the enemy. His all powerful spoken word. Pe is our mouths, supernaturally opened by God to give His children the "edge" or divine advantage through His almighty Word!

Those who receive and trust in Jesus will eventually move mountains... Selah.

The PE Prayer

Lord, I thank you for opening my mouth and empowering me with your word as I pray according to your will.
You have equipped me to eradicate darkness from my life, the lives of others and to prophesy change to negative circumstances we face.
I use my words of authority now to speak in agreement with Heaven concerning your plans for my life.

In Jesus Name.

Amen

The Eighteenth Letter

TSADDE

CHAPTER 18

TSADDE
God's Fish Hook

Righteous are You, O Lord, and upright are Your judgments.
Your testimonies, which You have commanded,
Are righteous and very faithful. My zeal has consumed me,
Because my enemies have forgotten Your words.
Your word is very pure; Therefore Your servant loves it.
I am small and despised, Yet I do not forget Your precepts.
Your righteousness is an everlasting righteousness,
And Your law is truth.
Trouble and anguish have overtaken me, Yet Your
commandments are my delights.
The righteousness of Your testimonies is everlasting;
Give me understanding, and I shall live.

Psalms 119 : 137 - 144

Jesus the Aleph Tav

Tsadde had a hieroglyphic of a fish hook when it was orig-inally drawn. This fish hook has a difference, it does not belong to a man, it belongs to God.

I would like to take you on an imaginary journey for a moment. Imagine you could see Heaven in all of its glory. You might be standing in a beautiful field full of flowers with your senses being invaded by gorgeous fragrances. In the distance, you catch a glimpse of a man in a boat on a huge sea. As you draw closer to him, you realise it is the Lord. You look into His eyes and see a tear-drop beginning to form. He looks just a little bit sad. He stands up and casts a giant hook into the sea. You look down and realise this is not water at all. It is not a lake. It is the earth! You watch intently, as Jesus grows to the size of a tall building and slowly pulls in a giant haul. Then you realise the purpose of this hook. It is not designed to catch fish, but men.

Did you manage to visualise that? I hope you did. This beau-tiful Hebrew letter carries within it, the very heart of God. It speaks of the Father's desire to catch and haul man back into His presence. In Tsadde we clearly see the lengths that God is willing to go to in order to save precious mankind. But alas, as in the days of Noah, men resist and fight. Much like a fish that has no intention of being caught. But still the great fisher of men continues His labour of love. Much like earthly anglers who work to provide for their families. God is working day and night without ceasing to bring man back to His love.

"For God so loved the world that He gave His only begotten Son, that whoever believes in Him should not perish but have everlasting life". John 3:16

God does not want anyone on earth to perish. I believe Jesus must shed real tears for people who die without receiving Him. His intentions were so pure. His sacrifice was so great. His suffering so terrible. What was the point of it all if mankind will not receive Him?

Prophetically speaking, if you can imagine the letter Tsadde in terms of a ministry, it would definitely have to be that of the Evangelist. We can see from scripture that evangelism stands at the forefront of Christ's ministry on the earth. When the Lord walked among us, He directly compared himself to many Hebrew letters as I have said before. However, you probably did not realise it but Tsadde, the fish hook was one of the first recorded. Cast your mind back to the following verse of scripture where the soon to be Apostles Simon and Andrew are called to the ministry. We saw it when we looked at Nun speaking of increase, this time we go to the book of Matthew:

Then He said to them, "Follow Me, and I will make you fishers of men." Matthew 4:19

Notice: Jesus said "I will make you fishers of men". He did not say I will teach you how to fish for men. He is saying 'If you have me, I am the hook that you can catch men with!' Hallelujah. I am Tsadde! My mission is to draw men out of the sea of the world and bring them safely back to my Father. This mission is expressed nowhere clearer than in the great book of Corinthians.

'Now all things are of God, who has reconciled us to Himself through Jesus Christ, and has given us the ministry of reconciliation, that is, that God was in Christ reconciling the world to Himself, not imputing their trespasses to them, and has committed to us the word of reconciliation'. 2 Corinthians 5:18.

We are God's family but the day when Adam sinned we lost personal access to Him. Jesus Christ (Yeshua) came to restore this access for us. When you and I accept the Lord, access to God's family is restored in Christ! This is such a great miracle for believers because we all become a part of His great plan of reconciliation. He saves us and we become a part of Tsadde. Now we appeal to others in the name of Christ. What is our new cry? Be reconciled to God. It is with the spirit of Tsadde, that the Holy Spirit drives us. Hook in hand, the Lord emboldens and motivates us to call everyone we can, to Christ.

David focuses much of this stanza on his personal pursuit for righteousness through the word of God. This is perfectly right thinking since the word is Christ Himself. For me, this clearly highlights his understanding of the letter Tsadde because in the Jewish mindset, to achieve perfect righteousness is to achieve salvation. The only problem was, some pious Jews like the Pharisees, took the issue too far. They believed they might achieve this righteousness by and through the law. This matter was addressed by Apostle Paul in his letter to the Galatians.

"Is the law then against the promises of God? Certainly not! For if there had been a law given which could have given life, truly righteousness would have been by the law". Galatians 3:21

In Christianity, righteousness is not achieved by any self effort but rather, it is received as a free gift. The Bible says "The law came through Moses, but grace and truth came through Jesus Christ". (John 1:17). We receive the gift of righteousness by His grace.

"For He made Him who knew no sin to be sin for us, that we might become the righteousness of God in Him". 2 Cor 5:21

I am the righteousness of God in Christ Jesus! I kept hearing preachers say these words over and over. It was as if it was a fashionable statement to make. For some reason, it really began to bother me. The truth is, the gift of God was so great and so free that my mind would not allow me to receive it. I even went on television broadcasts and warned people to be careful about saying it thoughtlessly because it sounds a little bit boastful. To be fair to my former self, there is a danger of people simply repeating what they have heard others say about a subject. Whereas, in reality they have not connected with the truth of the words they utter. Today, I have a good laugh at myself about it. Having connected with that truth I now ask myself, "What was I thinking"? A form of false humility was trying to rob me of the greatest blessing that Christ has ever given me. His righteousness. I read the scripture one day and suddenly I got it. It came alive for me because the word of God is a discerner of the thoughts and intentions of the heart. (Hebrews 4.12).

God made Him to be sin, who knew no sin so that we could become the righteousness of God in Him. This is why He did it. So that you and I could become... Selah!

There is nothing at all wrong with a Christian brother or sister making this claim. In fact, I now believe it is essential that we do! Jesus Christ died for the sins of all of mankind. He paid the ultimate price so that we should receive His righteousness. He went through hours of intense excruciating pain for us. He took scores of skin ripping lashes with a cat-o-nine-tails. According to the Prophet Isaiah, the chastisement of our peace was laid upon him and by His stripes, we are healed. Christ did all of this, so that we could be pronounced as the righteousness of God in Him. So if you are a believer in Jesus, you are part of the body of Christ. This means you are in Him. If you are in the body then

YOU ARE THE RIGHTEOUSNESS OF GOD IN CHRIST

I repented and asked God to forgive me for my foolish attitude. I am the righteousness of God in Christ Jesus. I will gladly say it for I do not want his sacrifice to be in vain.

In conclusion, Tsadde allows us to see God's heart towards man. Tsadde remind us of God's love for man and how that He is ever looking to bring us into His righteousness and presence through the sacrifice of His Son Jesus Christ, the Word.

Amen

The Prayer of Tsadde

Thank you Lord for coming from Heaven to earth to catch me. I declare that I am hooked forever to your presence.

Dear Lord, draw me nearer to you daily by your word and let me live in your presence forever.

Use my life as a hook to draw others to you so that they too can experience the joy of knowing you as I do.

Amen

The Nineteenth Letter

QOPH

CHAPTER 19

QOPH
The Back of the Head

*I cry out with my whole heart; Hear me, O Lord!
I will keep Your statutes. I cry out to You;
Save me, and I will keep Your testimonies.
I rise before the dawning of the morning, and cry for help;
I hope in Your word.
My eyes are awake through the night watches, that I may
meditate on Your word.
Hear my voice according to Your lovingkindness;
O Lord, revive me according to Your justice.
They draw near who follow after wickedness;
They are far from Your law.
You are near, O Lord, And all Your commandments are truth.
Concerning Your testimonies, I have known of old that You have
founded them forever.
Psalms 119 : 145 - 152*

We come now to a Hebrew letter which, at first glance gives us absolutely no clue as to its purpose or meaning. Though I cannot prove it, this letter was probably hieroglyph- ically drawn as a head seen from a side angle with special emphasis on the back portion. As strange as it may sound I submit to you that Qoph represents the back of the head. We arrived at this conclusion using a combination of Scripture, available historical judaical data and 'Sod" revelation from the Holy Ghost.

I can hear you asking what in the world could this strange defi- nition mean to us? And how in the world does this relate and connect us to Jesus Christ. What possible blessing or teaching does the understanding of such a thing afford to us who are born again? On this occasion the stanza itself holds the key. We must remember that David was fully cognisant about who and what he was writing within the separate stanzas of Psalm 119. In this section the Psalmist gives us a massive clue to the understanding and meaning of the letter Qoph.

We should begin by reading this stanza over again. I want you to notice the desperation it exudes. Did you notice how David cries three times to God for help? What do we learn from his appeals? He makes an appeal for God's loving kindness and then again for God's justice to be done. In verse 150 he confesses what he is actually concerned

Jesus the Aleph Tav

about. He says "They draw near who follow after wickedness; they are far from your law."

David is clearly concerned about his enemies. But why? Why should a warrior such as David be concerned about these haters? This was the same David who in his youth, slew Goliath. This was the David that they sang songs about. They said things like Saul has killed his thousands but David his ten thousands. David was a mighty warrior but yet something was keeping him up at night. It was the enemy that he could not see. His enemies were, as he said in his own writing "They that follow after wickedness".

Men and women of God I submit to you that we have the same common enemy that David had. These are not the ones which approach with guns, knives or weapons of any natural kind. Rather, these are they who work the works of darkness in secret. These are the ones we cannot see. Unless of course, we had as it were, eyes in the back of our heads! Can you begin to see it now?

By the way, It is well known in the world of combat sports that the most vulnerable part of the head is the back of it. Many a boxer has lost his title to a blow delivered to the base of the skull from which they could not recover.

Hebrew is the oldest language on earth. Therefore it is reasonable to suppose that the idiom "Eyes in the back of the head", is likely to have originated from the letter   Qoph.

It simply means to be fully aware of everything that is happening around you. Now we clearly begin to see the connection with Christ and particularly with the Holy Spirit. God has made provision for us both through His indwelling Spirit and the external presence of His mighty angels, whose job is to protect us from the things which we cannot see.

Discernment

At one point, I thought that Seva was suffering bouts of depression. She would go into a kind of melancholy mood, which she was not able to shake off. Whenever I would ask her if she was okay, she would answer "I am not sure". Then we noticed in the following days that some tragedy or situation would befall a member of her family. These were not depressions but rather prophetic insights into what was happening around her. Where David cries for help, we, by the great grace of God, give thanks because we already have the victory in Christ. That is a huge statement which will need to be corroborated by scripture. First of all, let us be clear about whom the head represents.

He is the image of the invisible God, the firstborn over all creation. For by Him all things were created that are in heaven and that are on earth, visible and invisible, whether thrones or dominions or principalities or powers. 'All things were created through Him and for Him. And He is before all things, and in Him all things consist. And He is the head of the body, the church, who is the beginning, the firstborn from the dead, that in all things He may have the pre-eminence'. Colossians 1 : 15-18

Clearly, the head is Christ. The one through whom all things were created. The walking, talking, living, eternal word. Note now the prayer which He prayed to the Father, for His disciples.

"I do not pray that You should take them out of the world, but that You should keep them from the evil one. They are not of the world, just as I am not of the world. Sanctify them by Your truth. Your word is truth". John 17 : 15-16

The Lord Jesus understood better than anyone about the devices of our mortal enemy. He knew that He could not leave His disciples in this world without having prayed for prophetic protection over their lives. With these words, Jesus Christ would create a sort of protective embassy for those who are part of the Kingdom of God. Members of this kingdom will legally receive advice, aid and where necessary, diplomatic immunity from the powers of this world. Qoph, believe it or not, is teaching us that as Christians, we are not subject to the lies, deceits and subjugations of the enemy. Especially the things which are done in secret as it were, behind our backs.

Some of course will say that such protection would have been afforded only to the disciples in the early church. They will tell you that today such miraculous protection no longer exists for the believer and that this promise has now been done away with. Whilst we respect all opinions within the body of Christ, I would urge that one to read on a little bit further, paying special attention to the following words;

"I do not pray for these alone, but also for those who will believe in Me through their word; that they all may be one, as You, Father, are in Me, and I in You; that they also may be one in Us, that the world may believe that You sent Me".
John 17:20-21

With this in mind, it is evident that cessation of God's protection for His children is impossible! It is as if the Lord foresaw this day in eternity past, knowing that His authority would someday be challenged. He, through this prayer, has set a precedent in the heavens which can never fail. As long as the earth remains, protection under this covenant is as sure to the believer in Christ, as the surety that tomorrow's sun will rise. Hallelujah.

Returning again to David's words in verse 150, "They draw near who follow after wickedness". However, he annuls their approach in the next verse, where he says " You ARE near oh Lord, and all your commandments are truth". When we reverse engineer this statement, David is sending a clear message to those in Christ today. When the enemy draws near with plans hatched in wickedness behind our backs, he will meet with a problem. The Lord is near to us! His commandments are truth for eternity.   Our enemies may draw near but God is even nearer!

In conclusion, the Lord's prayer of protection stands as an impenetrable shield against all of the machinations of the enemy.   Glory to God in the highest! Workers of witchcraft, and all manner of satanic and demoniacally birthed iniquity are stunted and discombobulated by the presence of God in our lives.

Qoph is so easy to overlook. It begins with a tickle but ends with a sledgehammer. Again, like the consecutive Ayin and Pe, Qoph and the 20th letter Resh are divinely connected by the Psalmist. Keep your thoughts on Qoph in the back of your head! Excuse the pun...

The Prayer of Qoph

Lord you see what we cannot see. You know what we cannot know but you reveal wonderful things to us through your Holy Spirit. Thank you for caring so much for us that you watch over our lives intently, keeping us safe from invisible enemies and dangerous pitfalls that we cannot see. Through your word we declare that even in our ignorance we are yet safe in Jesus Name.

Amen

Jesus the Aleph Tav

The Twentieth Letter

RESH

CHAPTER 20

RESH
The Head or the Highest

*Consider my affliction and deliver me, For I do not forget Your
law. Plead my cause and redeem me;
Revive me according to Your word.
Salvation is far from the wicked, For they do not seek Your
statutes. Great are Your tender mercies, O Lord;
Revive me according to Your judgments.
Many are my persecutors and my enemies, Yet I do not turn
from Your testimonies.
I see the treacherous, and am disgusted, Because they do not
keep Your word. Consider how I love Your precepts; Revive me, O
Lord, according to Your lovingkindness.
The entirety of Your word is truth, and every one of Your
righteous judgments endures forever.
Psalms 119 : 153 - 160*

When we think of the letter Resh, there is an immediate tendency to look upwards towards the heavens. this is because it symbolises the Head, the first or the highest. In fact I am going to take this one stage further. If you look at the shape of the letter you can begin to see a curvature that we might sometimes make with our hands, to imply that a matter is above our heads. As we prayed about Resh, this was revealed to me by the Lord. We are therefore going to define Resh as follows: **'Above the Head'.** Also referred to as Rosh, its meaning brings clarity to the feast of Rosh Hashannah (Trumpets), which is known as the HEAD OF THE YEAR. This is the high point of the Jewish calendar, which ushers in the high feasts. All of the feasts are important but "Rosh" makes it the Head of the year.

You may also notice that this stanza is filled with legal termi-nology. There is a reason for this. Now that we have reached the 20th letter, you may have noticed that David changes his style of speech with each letter. Each stanza has its own unique flow. This is one of the ways we understand that David knew and understood the meanings of each letter. Thereby he was able to scribe his thoughts about each one appropriately. These legal hints etch for us the corners of a jigsaw puzzle, which when completed, will provide rich insight into David's understanding of the letter.

Notice these terms; "Plead my cause", then "Revive me accord-ing to Your judgments". His words throughout revolve around testaments, laws and statutes. He ends the stanza with one of my favourite scriptures: "The entirety of Your word is truth, and every one of Your righteous judgments endures forever". David, in this moment, for some reason is wearing his barris-ter's wig. He sounds like he is making an appeal in a high court. Historical Judaism is steeped in law. Before there were Kings in Israel, there were Judges. These lawmakers were the first Hebrew rulers. Hebrew culture, to this day revolves around Jewish law which forms the root and centre of Jewish life and faith. For a Jew there is nothing higher than the law. Equally, As per the letter of the law, there is nothing and no-one higher than God. He is above the law because he wrote the law. He is the Resh.

There are laws which cover almost every aspect of Jewish lives. There are laws that cover the spiritual dimension also. It is to these laws that David primarily refers in this section. He is making his appeal to the highest court in the land. He is addressing the judge of all the earth and he is asking for an adjudication in his case.

A good example of spiritual laws can be found in a study of demonology in the Bible. Demons do not have free will where their work is concerned. They, like every other creature on planet earth must obey the laws of God. Most often when a demonic spirit enters into the life of a person, it will do so by way of a legal loophole. Good further reading matter on this subject would be a book called blessings and curses by Derek Prince. This is a must read for every believer. I, on the other hand would like to show you some important pictures of the total authority that God has over demon power. In the book of Job we see the head of the demons launching a verbal attack against Job. Whilst he is railing accusations at God, the deceiver must still apply to Him for permission in order to actually attack. (Job 1:9-12) Later we see several biblical instances where demons confronted Christ Himself.

When he saw Jesus from afar, he ran and worshipped Him. And he cried out with a loud voice and said, "What have I to do with You, Jesus, Son of the Most High God? I implore You by God that You do not torment me."
Mark 5:6-7

As I said earlier, everything in Judaic law is subject to the authority of God. The aforementioned could be described as a demonic counter claim. Amazingly, this demon spirit is actually attempting to bring Jesus before the highest authority to stop Him from tormenting him. Praise God my friends, the very presence of the authority of God in our lives is a tormenting presence to the realm of darkness. Hallelujah! That is something to praise God about. Resh is constantly reminding us that there is an authority above all authorities in Christ.

Have a look at the following scripture which gives us a sense of our Resh from both an earthly and heavenly perspective.

'He is the image of the invisible God, the firstborn over all creation. For by Him all things were created that are in heaven and that are on earth, visible and invisible, whether thrones or dominions or principalities or powers. All things were created through Him and for Him. And He is before all things, and in Him all things consist. And He is the head of the body, the church, who is the beginning, the firstborn from the dead, that in all things He may have the pre-eminence'.
Colossians 1 : 15-18.

Let us now go to the final verse of the stanza where we find a statement which it would be behove us to unlock a little further.

"The entirety of Your word is truth, And every one of Your righteous judgments endures forever".

I mentioned earlier that this is one of my favourite verses of scripture. These words are so simple, they are easily overlooked.

If you will take a moment to meditate upon them, they will become life changing, profound and miraculous. Having walked the Christian life for more than 27 years now, there is one factor that has become undeniable to me throughout this time;

The divine energy of God's word is able to overcome any negative fact that presents itself in your life.

If you did not get that the first time around, please read it again and again and again until your inner man is able to receive it. Have a good think about the word truth. It is a word used erroneously 98% of the time. I believe people confuse facts with truth.

FACT
A fact is something that is known to have happened or to exist, especially something for which proof exists, or about which there is information:

TRUTH
A truth is a fact or principle that is thought to be true by most people:

The former represents an intelligent effort to describe what truth is. However, the truth of the matter is that the English dictionary fails miserably in this attempt. David on the other hand does not fail in his definition. If you want to know what truth is the answer is simple.

Truth equals the word of God.

This is the highest authority in the heavens and in the earth and as such, it is automatically and irrevocably empowered with ability to overcome any fact in our lives.

In conclusion, the fact is, as believers we will face many negative circumstances. The way is never made easy for us. It is therefore vitally important that we maintain a correct perspective in so far as the word of God is concerned. In closing, if you can believe that the word of God has supreme authority over every aspect of your life, you are on track to become a recipient of God's divine miraculous judgement on earth.

Nothing is impossible for the one who will put his or her total trust in the word of God. It is the highest authority. I pray that Resh will forever serve as a reminder of this fact for you.

The Prayer of Resh

Lord, you are the highest authority in our lives. There is none above you in Heaven or in earth. Your decrees are final and there is no earthly authority that can overrule your judgements. When the enemy comes in, we lift up the standard of your word and we thank you for giving us victory in Jesus Name.

Amen

The Twenty-first Letter

Jesus the Aleph Tav

SHIN

Jesus the Aleph Tav

CHAPTER 21

SHIN
The Tooth - or Blessing

Princes persecute me without a cause, but my heart stands in awe of Your word.
I rejoice at Your word as one who finds great treasure.
I hate and abhor lying, but I love Your law.
Seven times a day I praise You, because of Your righteous judgments.
Great peace have those who love Your law, and nothing causes them to stumble.
Lord, I hope for Your salvation, and I do Your commandments.
My soul keeps Your testimonies, and I love them exceedingly. I keep Your precepts and Your testimonies,
For all my ways are before You.
Psalms 119 : 161 - 168

Jesus the Aleph Tav

SHIN The penultimate Hebrew letter is a very, very exciting one! This is especially for the born-again believer but also for the entire world. It carries the good news of the Gospel to all peoples of the earth. When we researched this letter, we were surprised at how little information was available about it. I believe its meanings were veiled to those who were writing about it. Apropos, there is something very important that I need to say at this point. If you have read all of these letters in succession you will by now have realised that much of the information we have presented has come directly from the Holy Spirit. Effectively our method was to study the Jewish perspective first, and then to overlay those foundations with Christian thought patterns. For some reason, Shin worked in the reverse. In order to see the beauty and value of the Hebraic meanings we had to start with Christ and work backwards.

I have listened to many Jewish Rabbis preach, usually around the time of the Jewish feasts. I am fascinated by the Jewish culture and enjoy keeping abreast of what is happening within the Jewish communities. Most of the time, when I listen to those Rabbis, I am often in agreement with the thought patterns presented. I even find myself saying amen quite often. That should not be surprising to read, since Christian and Jews do actually believe in the same God. I have found however, one huge difference between the two believing groups. I first noticed our uniqueness when I would listen to the closing remarks delivered by those Jewish Rabbis. You see with every respect to the Jewish community, at the end of the preaching I would often feel an awful emptiness. Yes, they presented hope but yet to me, I found in their delivery a greater sense of sadness. We must remember, that although we have the same God, they have not accepted Jesus as the Messiah as we Christians have.

"He came to His own, and His own did not receive Him. But as many as received Him, to them He gave the right (Power) to become children of God, to those who believe in His name: who were born, not of blood, nor of the will of the flesh, nor of the will of man, but of God".
John 1:11-13

The promise of His visitation remains painfully unfulfilled though amazingly and most patiently, they live in continued hope. Again, as a result, there is a certain sadness which seems to override the euphoria of the spoken message. The Christian message on the other hand is conclusively perfect. Come to Messiah is our cry. Come to the saviour of the world. Let Him cleanse you. Let Him take away your sin and bring you into eternal relationship and joy with God.

Shin to the Jew represents the molar tooth. It also speaks of the dual nature of man, both pre and after sin. You will notice that the letter has three prongs protruding upwards. There is also a small dot which appears above the shin, either above point 1 or 3. Dependent on where the dot appears, the sound changes from an 'S' symbolising sin, to a 'SH' sound which symbolises God's grace and blessing. Today, I believe the three prongs serve to remind us of the Holy Trinity. Now some may be a little offended by that term, insisting that there is no such word as trinity mentioned in the Bible. Whilst that is true, it is also true to note that there are other trinities in the Hebrew Torah and the Bible. The most recognisable being Abraham Isaac and Jacob. The number three, has always been a precious number for the Jewish people.

The real gem of understanding Shin, does not come from its hieroglyphic roots or its meaning. The real depth of under-standing will be gained from seeing it in application. There is a benediction used by the Jewish people which dates back to the very first high priest,who was Aaron. The benediction is known as "The priestly blessing". This blessing is still being practised every day by Jewish priests around the world. An integral part of this ritualistic blessing, is for the high priest to cover his head with his talit. (Shawl used for prayer). He then stretches his two hands towards the people. The congre-gation are advised to avert their eyes as it was supposed that the Shekinah (The presence and glory) of God will enter the room. The priests of old feared that people might be injured or even killed by such power. What an amazing thought! The high priests covered their heads by faith and the congregation also averted their eyes by faith. They were all believing that God's presence was about to enter the room!

What is the connection with the letter Shin? Visualise the high priest as he utters the words of the blessing you are about to read. His hands are lifted outside the veil of his talit. His fingers are divided into three groupings. The thumb being one group. The first and second fingers are held together. The third and little finger are also held together. When the hand is held in this way, it symbolically represents the letter Shin.

There is an interesting connection between Shin and the original series of **Star Trek**, which former viewers may be interested in. Leonard Nimoy (the actor who played the part of the fictional Vulcan character called Mr Spock) was of Jewish extraction. As a child he was taken to the synagogue regularly. On one such occasion, when the priestly blessing was being administered, he took a peek from under his father's talit. He saw the priest's hands stretched out amid the blessing. To his surprise, he lived to tell the tale. And tell it he did! Some years later, the writers were struggling to find a symbolic greeting for the character of Spock. Nimoy remembered what he had seen and suggested using the sign of the Shin. It was unanimously agreed by the program director Gene Roddenberry and two Jewish writers. As a result of this, the Hebrew letter Shin became synonymous with the Vulcan words "Live long and prosper!" I submit to you that Shin speaks primarily and ultimately of the blessing of the Lord which comes to us today through the Lord Jesus Christ!

'Blessed be the God and Father of our Lord Jesus Christ, who has blessed us with every spiritual blessing in the heavenly places in Christ,' Ephesians 1:3.

Do you see it! Every spiritual blessing in the heavenly places in Christ. This means that every spiritual blessing is now available through Jesus! Again we can venture into the book of Galatians and find more credible information on the exclusive blessing which comes to Christ.

And the Scripture, foreseeing that God would justify the Gentiles by faith, preached the gospel to Abraham beforehand, saying, "In you all the nations shall be blessed." So then those who are of faith are blessed with believing Abraham.
Galatians 3 : 8

So what is the Aaronic blessing? Where do we find the words of the priestly blessing and what do they mean to us today?

And the Lord spoke to Moses, saying: "Speak to Aaron and his sons, saying, 'This is the way you shall bless the children of Israel. Say to them: "The Lord bless you and keep you; The Lord make His face shine upon you, And be gracious to you; The Lord lift up His countenance upon you, And give you peace." ' "So they shall put My name on the children of Israel, and I will bless them." Numbers 6:22-27

My friends, the blessing is everything! Jews and Christians are fully aware of this fact. If the Lord God has put His blessing on you, your life on earth will be amazing. You will prosper and be in health. Everyone must face challenges in this world. However, blessed people never have to face the challenges alone. David writes in verse 165, "Great peace have those who love your law, and nothing causes them to stumble". The blessing of the Lord brings stability and inner peace. The recipients walk in constant awareness of the fact that they are blessed of God.

Certain cultures seem to understand this word blessing more than others. There is one often overlooked factor about the blessing which in all cases concur. There are many symbolic practices which may accompany and embellish the various benedictions. However, all blessings are imparted ultimately by way of the spoken word.

In conclusion, until Christ came, the Abrahamic Hebraic people were the carriers of the blessing of the Lord in the earth. Passed from generation to generation, high priest to high priest. Father to Son. The only way to receive God's blessing was to be somehow connected with them. Today, God has extended that blessing to the entire human race through the love and sacrifice of his son Jesus Christ. Shin is the Hebrew letter that connects all the dots for us. Its three prongs now symbolise the Father, the Son and the Holy Spirit. This ancient Hebrew letter, Shin, depicted the way to the blessing of God. Thousands of years before the 'Trinity' would become known through the appearance of Jesus Christ, The letter Shin openly declared His coming and blessing. Selah!

**Jesus Christ is the SHIN
Extending His hands of blessing
Outside the ripped veil, to all of mankind.**

Jesus the Aleph Tav

SHIN'S Prayer

"The Lord bless you and keep you; The Lord make His face shine upon you, And be gracious to you; The Lord lift up His countenance upon you, And give you peace."

Heavenly Father we thank you for the blessing of your son Christ Jesus and all that He imparts to us as your children. According to Ephesians 1:3 we receive every Spiritual blessing in Heavenly places in Christ Jesus. Thank you for allowing us in Christ to come boldly before your throne of grace so that we can receive all you have for us in Jesus Name. We receive your blessing now.

Amen

Twenty two - The Final Letter

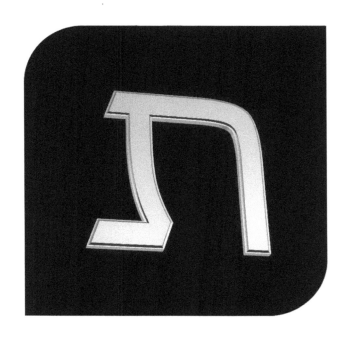

TAV

CHAPTER 22

TAV
The mark of the Cross

Let my cry come before You, O Lord;
Give me understanding according to Your word.
Let my supplication come before You;
Deliver me according to Your word.
My lips shall utter praise,For You teach me Your statutes.
My tongue shall speak of Your word,
For all Your commandments are righteousness.
Let Your hand become my help, For I have chosen Your precepts.
I long for Your salvation, O Lord, And Your law is my delight.
Let my soul live, and it shall praise You; And let Your judgments
help me.
I have gone astray like a lost sheep; Seek Your servant,
For I do not forget Your commandments.
Psalms 119 : 161 - 168

TAV is the final letter of the Hebrew alphabet. It is often defined as the cross shaped mark. However, it does not resemble a cross as we know it today. I think it is worth noting that the cross of Christ really consisted of a crossbeam. (The one which Christ would have carried to Calvary). This would have been hung on a support of some kind. Oft-times crucifixions took place on a tree or between two adjacent trees.

The first mention of the word Tav occurs in the book of Genesis chapter 4. At this point, Adam's first son Cain is on the run having slain his brother Abel. God had put him out of the garden because of his sin. Cain complained to God saying now whoever finds me will slay me!

And the Lord said to him, "Therefore, whoever kills Cain, vengeance shall be taken on him sevenfold." And the Lord set a mark on Cain, lest anyone finding him should kill him. Genesis 4:15

With this action, Almighty God prophetically declares the complete gospel. Cain is guilty of judgement. But God does not allow him to perish. Instead He sets the mark of the cross upon him and through that mark, Cain comes under divine protection from God.

Look at the similarities. We are born and shaped in iniquity. We are guilty yet the chastisement of our peace is laid on Christ. God sent His son to die on the cross. Through Calvary our sins are forgiven so that we should not perish. We are protected and given eternal life.   The cross of Jesus Christ is a cross of grace.

**Tav is the mark of grace, saying
You shall not die but LIVE.**

In the opening chapter of the book of Revelation, Jesus Christ introduces himself to the John, the Apostle. The very first thing He says is;

*"I am the Alpha and the Omega, the first and the last",
Revelation 1:8*

Or was it? In reality, we know that both Jesus and John spoke in the ancient dialect of Hebrew known as Aramaic. As such, the words used would not have been Greek. They would have been Hebrew. I submit to you that Christ actually introduces Himself as the Aleph and Tav. These words were later translated into Greek. Why is this important? When we translate these letters into other languages we lose some of the original colour and meaning applied to the letter by God. That is one of the reasons why this book has been written.

Just think, this was the first sentence that Christ spoke to John on the Isle of Patmos. These words were designed to both grab and keep John's attention. They were hugely important.

The Aleph Tav

There are three ways that we can interpret the words of Christ concerning the Aleph Tav.

1. A reference to Time - The phrase can be looked at as a reference to time especially since Jesus followed up the statement with the words 'the first and the last'. We could take this to mean that like God the Father, Christ sees the end from the beginning. Whilst this is a wonderful sentiment, thoroughly worthy of Jesus Christ, we should handle this definition carefully since Christ Himself also said that there were some aspects of the future that only the Father knew.

"But of that day and hour no one knows, not even the angels of heaven, but My Father only. Matthew 24:36

2. The Word in Flesh - As you have now completed the

previous 21 chapters with me, the second definition should be obvious to you. Christ is saying I am every single letter and definition from Aleph to Tav.

I am Aleph, Beth, Gimel, Daleth, He etc. I am the Word of God personified. I am the Word that became flesh and dwelt among you. I am the walking talking representation of God on earth. I am The Word. I was with God in the beginning. I am that very Word which was God. Amen.

The complete study of the Hebrew letters caused us to see revelation in a whole new light. For me, this is the most probable interpretation of His opening words to John. However, remember the Pardes (Hebrew exegesis teaching) that we talked about earlier in the book. There is absolutely no need to jettison one thought in order to accept the other. All of the revelations sit handsomely together without conflicting with each other.

3. The Aleph Tav - There is a third interpretation, which when seen from a Hebraic perspective is also extremely viable. To understand this, we must delve yet further into the Hebraic culture and teaching. Jewish scholars sometimes combine the two letters, Tav & Aleph so that they appear co-joined. When written this way, the Aleph Tav becomes a unique symbol and title in itself. Moses, Abraham, Isaac and Jacob are all beneficiaries of the Aleph Tav title. When writing about these forefathers in the faith, the Hebrews would place the symbol directly after their names. In this light, the symbol takes on the character of a qualification or accolade. Much in the same way as we might put the letters PH.D. after a doctor's name. In this case, the meaning is very profound. The symbol is basically denoting that these individuals were perfectly in covenant with God the Father. His attributes were seen through them. They were co-joined with the Father. In more modern vernacular we would call them types of Christ. So who ultimately would have the right to make such a declaration about Himself? There is none more qualified than Jesus Christ.

To coin a phrase King David really makes a meal of this stanza. He seems to cover quite a lot of ground. The final section appears to be an homage to the previous 21 letters. I think this may have been his intention, having guided us through all of the Hebrew alphabet faithfully to this point. I would like to draw our attention to his closing comments in verse 176.

I have gone astray like a lost sheep; seek your servant, for I do not forget your commandments.

Jesus the Aleph Tav

What a very strange way to end such a powerful Psalm. Is David making an admission of his state of sin? After having taken us to the very heights of revelation in the word. Is he finally leaving us without hope? After all of the encouragement that David has given us, are we really to believe that his final state is to be totally astray from God? At first glance, It would be very easy to think this way especially if you did not have an understanding of the meaning of Tav. However, if we cast our minds back to the definition given at the beginning of this chapter, it is clearer to see David's intention. David is saying although I have gone astray like a lost sheep, I have been marked by you so I know you will seek your servant. I cannot be lost as long as I have your mark upon me. This is a reference to Tav, which like a modern electronic tag, assures him of safety, even when he is in error. David ends the 22nd letter with the most beautiful analogy of the Shepherd seeking the lost sheep of His flock. This picture is overflowing with Christ-likeness.

He, after all is the good Shepherd, who will leave the 99 in order to find that one which was lost. Selah.

In conclusion, "I am the Alpha and Omega, the beginning and the end, the first and the last". Christ was not speaking in Greek, therefore we know that what He actually said was "I am the Aleph Tav". We take this to mean that Christ was saying look at the Hebrew Alphabet and study its stanzas, you will find me there! We have looked together and studied together. We know you will benefit from new levels of revelation through the time we have spent together. We leave you in the hands of the Fathers love, In Yeshua, Christ, Jesus, Amen.

'In the beginning was the Word, and the Word was with God, and the Word was God. He was in the beginning with God. All things were made through Him, and without Him nothing was made that was made. In Him was life, and the life was the light of men. And the light shines in the darkness, and the darkness did not comprehend it'. John 1:1-5

'And the Word became flesh and dwelt among us, and we beheld His glory, the glory as of the only begotten of the Father, full of grace and truth'. John 1:14

Christ is the word! His story is every revelation found in the Aleph Tav. His presence in our lives bears witness to it.

You search the Scriptures, for in them you think you have eternal life; and these are they which testify of Me. John 5:39

Jesus the Aleph Tav

Prayer of Tav

Heavenly Father, we declare today that we are marked through your word and the presence of the Lord Jesus Christ in our lives. Thank you for your covenant towards us and for the boundless benefits we receive through it. As we close our prayer and study, we give you thanks for your kindness and grace in the name of the Father, Son and the Holy Spirit.

Amen

Glossary of terms

GLOSSARY

Pardes

Jewish Exegesis method that helps us to broaden our understanding of the word of God.

Have you ever wondered why several people in a room reading the same scriptures yet all are receiving slightly or completely different interpretations on the subject? Perhaps the answer can be found in the ancient Jewish PARDES concept.

A study of Jewish exegesis suggests that there are four basic ways in which to interpret the scriptures and that all are acceptable and correct dependent upon your point of view. In the movie Fiddler on the roof, there are several "Pardes" moments occurring each time the main character played by Topov says "But then again"...

PARDES is a simple acronym that helps us to remember the four distinct thought patterns involved in the interpretation of all scripture. As with anything that appears to be new to our understanding, my advice is that you seek the Lord before utilising this study system. This is so that He may lead you into using it in a manner that brings glory to Him.

The definition of PARDES is as follows: "Pardes" refers to (types of) approaches to biblical exegesis in rabbinic Judaism (or - simpler -interpretation of text in Torah study). The term, sometimes also spelled PaRDeS, is an acronym formed from the name initials of the following four approaches:

Peshat — *"plain" ("simple") or the direct meaning*

Remez — *"hints" or the deep (allegoric: hidden or symbolic) meaning beyond just the literal sense.*

Derash — *from Hebrew darash: "inquire" ("seek") — the comparative (midrashic) meaning, as given through similar occurrences.*

Sod — *(pronounced with a long O as in 'bone') — "secret" ("mystery") or the mystical meaning, as given through inspiration or revelation.*

Each type of "Pardes" interpretation examines the extended meaning of a text. As a general rule, the extended meaning never contradicts the base meaning.

Peshat

The Peshat means the plain or contextual meaning of the text. This does not mean that you cannot draw revelation from it. It simply represents the plain truth. An example of this would be: Scriptures that use the term "atonement", meaning reconciliation could be simplified by breaking the word down into AT ONE MENT. It is a plain truth, full of deep revelation!

Remez

The Remez could represent an allegorical meaning like the Pool of Bethesda found in John 5:2 the five porches mentioned could be representing the number of grace explaining why people were being healed there. The number of porches was the hint that leads us to the revelation.

Derash

Derash - The Derash is very exciting because it requires us to seek the Lord for the hidden meaning of one scripture by comparing it with another. These revelations are made available to us by seeking the Lord's face and wisdom. This is probably the primary way in which the Lord speaks to me! Often I have simply sat and enquired of the Lord about something, and then sat quietly waiting for Him to speak. As I would meditate on the verse of scripture another will just show up in my inner consciousness. As I mediate on the two, a bridge forms. This is the midrashic bridge of truth applied by the Spirit of truth, between the two verses

Sod

Sod - For me represents the direct injection of revelation from Yahweh God the Father. Sod revelation will never contradict the Bible and will always arrive with an inner witness to assure you of its integrity. The best example of Sod for me, could be found in Matthew 16.

He saith unto them, "But whom say ye that I am"? And Simon Peter answered and said, Thou art the Christ, the Son of the living God. And Jesus answered and said unto him, "Blessed art thou, Simon Barjona: for flesh and blood hath not revealed it unto thee, but my Father which is in heaven". Mat 16:15 -19

If the Father revealed a word directly to the heart of Peter, prior to Christ going to the cross and the subsequent shedding of the Holy Spirit in our hearts. How much more for us who have the inner witness of the Lord in us! We should both pray and expect Sod revelation because we are Sons of the most high God.

We have the Holy Spirit,
Why do we need "Pardes"?

Firstly let me say that I believe that as Christians we must always look to the Holy Spirit for our guidance through scripture.

I also believe that the Jewish people were given certain principles and directives from God which seem to have been lost from our westernised version of the faith. I have often come across believers who dogmatically state their interpretation of a scripture, completely ignoring anyone else's interpretations. When I heard about "Pardes" I was delighted, simply because I now have a tool that I can use to bring a sense of peace when dual interpretations seem to be present.

Hebrew letters and their English equivalents

name	letter	pronunciation	
Aleph	א	silent	ʾ
Bet	ב	b, v	
Gimel	ג	g	
Dalet	ד	d	
Hey	ה	h	
Waw	ו	w	
Zayin	ז	z	
Het	ח	h	ẖ
Tet	ט	t	ṭ
Yod	י	y	
Kaph	ך כ	k, kh	
Lamed	ל	l	
Mem	ם מ	m	
Nun	ן נ	n	
Samekh	ס	s	
Ayin	ע	silent	ʿ
Peh	ף פ	p, ph	
Tsade	ץ צ	ts	ṣ
Qoph	ק	q	
Resh	ר	r	
Shin	ש	s, sh	š
Taw	ת	t	

Jesus the Aleph Tav

THANKS & DEDICATIONS

Firstly I would like to give thanks to God for his ever unfolding grace and kindness in my life..

Thanks to Seva Jackman (my wife) who spent six months researching these Hebrew letters with me. We also enjoyed co-presenting Word & Prayer together. Also to my dear daughter Janah, I pray that you will find enlightenment from God in the words of this book. Finally to my darling Mum, Maria. Thank you for always believing in and encouraging me.

PERMISSIONS

ABOUT THE AUTHOR

Born in the east end of London, Hugh Alexander Jackman became an entrepreneur in the worlds of fashion, beauty and music production. Then an encounter with the Lord Jesus changed his world. Early in his Christian life, the Lord opened a wonderful door which propelled Hugh into national Christian television. He aided in the early development and growth of three Christian TV stations including God TV, Dove Vision and Revelation TV. In 2006, He also launched a new TV network called Faithglobe.tv. After this he spent many years as a presenter of the popular Bible Study program on Revelation TV. Ministerially, Hugh is a 'Seer'.

Hugh is a public speaker. He truly enjoys ministering the word of God in churches of all sizes with signs and wonders following. He also produces and presents independent TV programs including Spirit and Life and New Faith Generation. His mission is to bring focus to the present reality of Jesus Christ, drawing as many as he can to the Kingdom of God through the creation of Christian Messianic media. Other materials are available at Hugh Jackman Ministries and Spirit & Life Ministries websites:

www.hughjackman.org.uk
www.spiritandlife.org.uk

Jesus the Aleph Tav

Milton Keynes UK
Ingram Content Group UK Ltd.
UKHW011455260824
447446UK00015B/1126